FAB BOARDING CATTERY INFORMATION SERVICE

feline advisory bureau

Offering advice, practical training courses and key information for running a quality boarding cattery

BOARDING CATTERY
CONSTRUCTION
AND MANAGEMENT MANUAL
(4th edn) by Sophie Hamilton Moore and Caryl Cruickshank

The definitive manual on building and running a first class boarding cattery based on 30 years of experience in raising the standards of boarding catteries and incorporating the most up-to-date information on the health and welfare of cats.

TRAINING COURSES

Practical intense six day residential courses with teaching on a one to one basis. Advice is also available on choosing a quarantine cattery. **The FAB Boarding Cattery Information Service** is a branch of the Feline Advisory Bureau, a charity dedicated to improving the health and welfare of cats.

FAB Boarding Cattery Information Service,
1 Church Close, Orcheston, Salisbury, Wiltshire
SP3 4RP Tel/Fax 01980 621201

Find out about membership and benefit from FAB's expertise by contacting:
FAB Taeselbury, High Street, Tisbury, Wiltshire SP3 6LD.
Tel 01747 871872, Fax 01747 871873
Registered charity no 254641

Animal Care College

Ascot House
High Street, Ascot
Berkshire SL5 7G
Tel: 01344 28269
Fax: 01344 22771

The Animal Care College has been delivering open learning courses on all aspects of animal care since 1980.

They include:–

- Diploma of Kennel Management
- National Small Animal Care Certificate (NVQ Levels 1–3)
- Diploma in Pet Bereavement Counselling
- Grooming Theory
- Veterinary Nursing
- Understanding the Canine/Human Interface
- Understanding the Feline/Human Interface

Contact the Registrar at the College for full details of all courses

Running Your Own

BOARDING KENNELS

Revised Second Edition

Sheila Zabawa

KOGAN
PAGE

First published in 1985
Reprinted with revisions 1986, 1988
Second edition 1992
Reprinted with revisions 1997
Reprinted 1999

Kogan Page Limited
120 Pentonville Road
London N1 9JN

© Sheila Zabawa 1985, 1992

British Library Cataloguing in Publication Data

A CIP record for this book is available from the British Library.

ISBN 0-7494-0595-3

Printed and bound in Great Britain by Biddles Limited, Guildford and King's Lynn

Contents

Acknowledgements   6

Foreword   7
    by David Cavill, Principal, Bell Mead
    Kennel Staff Training College

1. Facing the Facts   9
    A second career 11; Gaining the
    knowledge 11; Animal nursing 13; Practical
    preparation 13; Formal training 14; The
    boarding cattery 14; Taking responsibility
    for animals 15

2. Finding Your Property   17
    Location 17; Boarding capacity 19;
    Quarantine kennels 19; Starting a new
    business 20; Buying an existing business
    21; Boarding fees and licences 24; Owner's
    accommodation 25; Financial enquiries
    26

3. Professional and Other Advice   28
    Property 28; Raising finance 29; Business
    structure 30; Free advice 31; Solicitor
    32; Insurance 33; Accounting 35; Local
    officials 35

4. Finance and Running Costs   37
    Income 37; Outgoings 37; Value added tax
    39; Keeping accounts 39; Getting the best
    deals 40; Updating your knowledge 40

5. Laws and Orders:
Statutory Requirements   42
    The Animal Boarding Establishments Act
    1963 42; The Diseases of Animals (Approved
    Disinfectants) Order 1978 (amended 1991)
    46; Licensing authorities 46; Liability for
    damage 47; Retail trading 47; Terms for
    boarding 49

6. Health Matters   52
Kennel cleaning 53; Insecticides 60;
Exterior cleaning 61; Sterilisation of
feeding and drinking bowls 62; Disposal
problems 62; Human considerations
67; Safety first 68; Zoonoses and other
ailments 70; Dangerous dogs 76

7. Feeding the Boarders   79
Types of pet food 80; Canned food 82;
Semi-moist food 82; Complete dry food
82; Vacuum packed meats 83; Deep frozen
food 84; Boil-in-the-bag food 84; Complete
dry diets for dogs and cats 85; Self-feeding
88; Conclusion 89

8. The Daily Round   90
Exercise 90; Cleaning routine 91;
Mealtimes 92; The kennel kitchen 93;
Beds and towels 94; Taking stock 95;
Heating 95; Health record cards 95;
Grooming 96; Reception area 97;
Arrivals and departures 99; Enquiries 100;
Problems which may be encountered 100;
Veterinary surgeons' visits 104; Final check
105

9. Kennel Staff   106
Accommodation 107; Staff training 108;
Checking in 109; Income tax and National
Insurance 109; Contract of employment
110; Health hazards 111

10. Kennel Buildings   112
Adapting existing property 112; New
designs 113; Conventional kennel
accommodation 113; Heating 122

11. Fanfare   124
Trade sign 124; Advertising 124; Telephone
enquiries 126; Stationery 127; Local
activities 128; Unlicensed competition
130

12. Expanding Your Business   132
Increased capacity 132; Grooming services
133; Product sales 134; Puppy rearing 135;
Quarantine kennels 136

Appendix **139**
Useful addresses 139; Further reading
142

Index **144**

Acknowledgements

I gratefully acknowledge the help, encouragement and advice given me by many people including Mr David Cavill of the Bellmead Kennel Staff Training College, the late Miss S M Hamilton Moore, former Boarding Cattery Officer of the Feline Advisory Bureau, Mr Trevor Turner, MRCVS, Dr Alan Walker, Mr Vincent Hogan and Mr William Moores of *Our Dogs*, Mr Tony Ellis and Miss Carol Andrews of *Kennel and Cattery Management*, and Mr Jerry Brownlee of Pet Plan Insurance Ltd. My particular thanks go to Mrs Brenda Judson, Mrs Jill Ashwick, and also to Wendy and Graham Stephens of Arden Grange International Quarantine and Boarding Kennels for their practical advice as experienced kennel owners. I am extremely grateful to Monica and David Marshall for allowing me to share their initiation into the world of boarding kennel ownership, and who have continued to make me welcome on frequent visits to their now well established kennel business.

Drawings by Sharon Garrick.

Sheila Zabawa
September 1991

Foreword

by David Cavill, FInst D, MBIM
Principal, Bell Mead Kennel Staff Training College

The three and a half thousand boarding kennels are the major element of animal care and an increasingly important element of the leisure sector of the UK economy. As people's free time increases along with their disposable income they are not only more likely to have pets as members of the family but will need to find a suitable home for them while on holiday.

Not so many years ago families had only one holiday a year. Now they may go away three or four times, in addition to the occasional long weekend. At the same time, although the number of spaces at boarding kennels is rising gradually, this is almost entirely due to the expansion of kennels already recognised by local authorities. Gaining planning permission for a new dog boarding kennel is quite difficult so the market is expanding faster than the total capacity is increasing.

The industry copes because the occupation rate of kennels is now much higher than it once was. As families are spreading their holidays over the whole year most boarding kennels, which once could virtually close down for three or four months each year without it having a major effect on their income, are finding there is never a week when they are empty. Added to the greater occupancy are the opportunities for food and equipment sales, grooming and even animal taxi services. A good boarding kennel is a sound investment and can provide a reasonable income. No wonder there is a constant demand for licensed kennels through the specialist agencies. It sounds like a very good deal. Living in the country, working at home with a regular income, surrounded by loving animals – what more could you want?

Anyone can buy a kennel. No qualifications are needed and, although this is true of other businesses, few are so small that they do not come with employees who already know the ropes. With kennels the owners are on their own, with perhaps a couple of untrained youngsters, and the care of animals belonging to other people can be an awesome responsibility. They are living creatures and must be housed, fed, cleaned and cared for to the highest standards. The good news is Sheila Zabawa's wonderful guide, this entirely new edition of *Running Your Own Boarding Kennels*.

The book cannot replace the hard work but it can make sure that you go into a fascinating, satisfying and absorbing business with your eyes open. Sheila guides you through the maze of law, welfare, care, CoSSH, H&S, feeding, staffing and finance with all the confidence you would expect from someone who is well acquainted with the environment she describes. Her advice is based on experience and she deals methodically and sensibly with both the major and minor problems of caring for animals, and buying, developing and managing a business. This book can save you both money and worry – do not consider buying a boarding kennel unless you have read it thoroughly.

Chapter 1

Facing the Facts

Before considering the purchase of a boarding kennel it is important to ask yourself and your family, 'Will life in a boarding kennel suit us?' It is even more important to pause for thought and endeavour to give yourselves an honest answer, for many people wishing to enter the kennel business have had little or no experience of small animal boarding establishments and therefore have not very much on which to base their answers. It is an occupation of great responsibility involving the complete care of other people's pets; a kind, caring and understanding attitude towards animals is essential.

Dogs and cats, and possibly some other small animals, become residents of a boarding kennel intermittently for varying periods. The kennel owners live there permanently, and although their personal accommodation is somewhat more spacious, they also face certain restrictions when assuming a 24 hours a day, seven days a week, responsibility for their clients' pets. Naturally, there are compensations and all aspects need to be weighed carefully before embarking on a venture which is demanding both in capital investment and physical endurance, but which can be highly rewarding in terms of satisfaction provided the kennel owners are suited to their work, and can make the most of its advantages and tolerate its disadvantages.

Boarding kennels are extremely individual businesses offering self-employment, freedom from a deskbound job, an outdoor life and, it would seem, they could be entering a growth period as people tend to take more holidays than in the past and therefore need boarding facilities for their pets more frequently. This is also an era in which restrictions on dogs have become more severe. Shops, beaches, hotels, caravan parks, self-catering holiday flats or chalets and public parks have become 'off limits' to dogs, or are so stringent in their restrictions that visitors taking their pets into strange areas find their own vacations spoiled. It is far better for the family pet to go to his own holiday camp – your boarding kennel! Many boarding kennel owners are now finding that they have some bookings all the year round as winter holidays are becoming universally popular, and weekend breaks, which are extensively advertised, are attracting people who have the leisure to enjoy them.

Nevertheless, some parts of the year will definitely see the kennels more empty than others and careful planning is needed in the early days of ownership to cover the lean periods financially. Freedom from constant clerical work does not mean that there are no desk jobs at all. Accounts must be kept, bookings made, a register of boarders maintained and, particularly while you are gaining experience, investigations into all aspects of running the business profitably need to be continued. The outdoor life, which can be very enjoyable when the weather is beautiful, must be endured when it is inclement beyond description; it is not easy to enjoy working outside in torrents of rain but the basic tasks still need to be done.

A flair for DIY is a definite asset to any boarding kennel owner. There are always maintenance and alteration jobs, as some dogs while away their happy holiday hours destroying whatever their teeth and claws can reach, and there is usually something in a kennel block which might be better for some modification. If a kennel owner is a competent plumbing and heating engineer and an expert in drains, as well as a capable electrician, so much the better! However, many folk of slight physical strength and deficient in DIY aptitude become extremely successful boarding kennel owners. Profitable kennel ownership may well be a triumph over adversity, and what constitutes a serious problem for one owner may be a mere bagatelle for the next.

Boarding establishments for family pets are sometimes part of a breeding and exhibiting kennel. Usually, dog or cat breeding or exhibiting has led the owner into the boarding business. In such cases the owner may have acquired considerable experience of animals in a kennel environment before assuming the care of other people's pets. However, people who wish to follow the exhibition lure will find that show dates conflict with the busiest boarding season, necessitating complicated staffing arrangements and, though exhibiting at dog or cat shows can be a compelling interest, it is not in itself a paying occupation. It costs money, even for the glory of winning at prestigious shows. Show entries can be expensive, prize money nil and travel costs exorbitant, not to mention extra staff salaries if members of the family are not available to cope on the home front while others are away at shows. Remember that pet owners, when leaving or collecting their dogs and cats, expect to be met by competent adults; if a boarding kennel owner is not available to attend to the clients personally, it is essential for the confidence of the clients and the goodwill of the establishment that whoever meets them makes a good impression. Can you and your family give yourselves wholeheartedly to the business, particularly in the early days of ownership?

A second career

Many people come into the boarding kennel business as a second career with the advantage of business or professional experience and training, and a certain maturity. Boarding kennel ownership attracts some people already qualified in animal care. Veterinary surgeons sometimes own kennels and obviously have many professional advantages; Registered Veterinary Nurses are often interested in kennel ownership and again have definite advantages of training and experience. Members of the armed forces, many of whom retire from the services in their middle years, quite frequently find the ownership of animal boarding establishments an interesting and practical pursuit. Years of training, discipline and an outdoor life, plus dependability and self-sufficiency, are a commendable background. Men and women from all walks of life are interested in animal care, and many find that the boarding kennel business appears to offer them the ideal occupation.

Those choosing kennel ownership as a second career usually have ample time to consider possibilities and prepare for the tasks involved. When life has not previously included specific training in animal welfare, how should prospective kennellers proceed?

Gaining the knowledge

It would be wise to obtain some practical experience and to become as well informed as possible on all subjects relevant to small animal care. How can this be achieved? It can be done by benefiting from the peripheral activities connected with the exhibition community, which is closer knit than the boarding kennel world.

The exhibition scene, through its excellent publications, provides some necessary background information and general reading material of interest to intending kennel owners. In particular, the weekly canine journals print up-to-date news concerning changes in legislation, and carry a wealth of advertising material which is most useful.

One monthly journal, *Kennel and Cattery Management*, is aimed specifically at the boarding trade and contains informative articles on all subjects relating to small animal boarding. Other canine and feline journals encompass the show and breeding world as well as publishing items of interest for boarding kennel owners. People who plan to become the owners of boarding establishments should certainly become regular readers of such weekly papers as *Dog World*, *Our Dogs*, and its sister magazine *Cats*, all obtainable to order from newsagents nationwide. *Dogs Monthly* and *Cat World* are also available from newsagents.

Intending boarding kennel owners, though they may not be interested in showing dogs themselves, should read the forthcoming show announcements in *Our Dogs* and *Dog World* if only to be aware of what is going on in their own area. They give details of shows nationwide for exhibitors making entries in advance, and list current events for intending spectators. So many people have the false idea that Crufts is the only dog show! There is sure to be a dog or cat show at some time in your present neighbourhood, or at least within a reasonable travelling distance. Attending local shows could help you to become more familiar with breeds of dogs and cats you may never before have encountered but might at some time board. Championship dog and cat shows attract the highest number of entries and of trade stands dealing in kennel necessities. The trade sections are worth visiting too. Separate trade fairs are also interesting, and advertisements for them will be found in the weekly dog press and in the monthly magazines, *Pet Product Marketing* and *Pet Business World*.

The noise factor

Dogs bark! A superfluous statement? Not really. One of the most important questions intending boarding kennel owners must ask themselves is, 'Can I tolerate a high level of noise?' Naturally, barking cannot be prevented and though good management may keep the noise level in check there will be some extremely noisy spells. Noise is a stress factor and can be very wearing at times. For some people it is unbearable. Boarding kennel owners must learn to live with it, or live elsewhere.

Unpleasant smells and dirty jobs

Boarding kennel owners also have to accept other unavoidable facts: kennel work is very strenuous, and the dirty and tiresome jobs, as well as the more enjoyable tasks, have to be done.

Can you tolerate nasty smells? This question has to be answered truthfully. Although you may consider that all household pets will be house-trained, your kennel routine will be different from their home surroundings and the dogs will not understand at first why they have been handed over to you. Also, the smell of other dogs may set off their reactions and home toilet training may be temporarily forgotten.

There will be dirty kennels to cope with on most days, and in quarantine, where dogs are confine to the same kennel and adjoining exercise area for the duration of their detention, there will always be dirty kennels to clean and disinfect. If you cannot face unpleasant smells you cannot face a kennel job, and you must be honest with yourself about these basic problems.

Animal nursing

Although the boarding kennel business attracts people who have had animal nursing experience, many newcomers to the trade will have had no dealings with sick animals, or even those with chronic conditions needing regular medication. Unless a boarding kennel owner is competent in caring for ailing animals he must recommend their owners to another kennel or to a veterinary surgeon. There are dogs which are diabetic and need daily treatment; dogs with a pancreatic deficiency may need a special diet routine; there are dogs with kidney disorders, very young dogs, aged dogs . . . all possible subjects for nursing care. Can you give this? Could you learn to give such care? Giving pills to dogs and cats is not always easy.

Practical preparation

The acquisition of practical experience of kennel work for a second career may not be easy unless you are prepared to sacrifice some of your leisure to work in a voluntary capacity, perhaps for an animal charity. This could be well worth doing for many reasons. Contact your local branch of the Royal Society for the Prevention of Cruelty to Animals, or the National Canine Defence League, and enquire whether they could use a helping hand. There may possibly be an independent local animal sanctuary needing help; consult the Yellow Pages under 'Boarding Kennels' for information.

It may be possible to help out voluntarily at a local boarding kennel or cattery, or perhaps you have friends already established in the business who would be pleased to assist with your indoctrination. It would be a good plan to see as many kennels as possible, but remember that kennel owners are extremely busy people; they are working when they may seem to you to be simply standing and watching! Show courtesy and consideration, and always make an appointment in advance. Be as understanding of them as you hope others will be of you in the future. Friends who are established owners are in a position to point out small matters of importance that the uninitiated may not otherwise see.

Formal training

Fortunately, recent years have seen great strides in opportunities for people interested in working with animals in the boarding environment to gain formal education. They can now study for the Diploma of Kennel Management which is a Canine Studies Institute course organised and administered by RTC Associates, Red Tile Cottage, London Road, Bracknell, Berkshire RG12 6QN; the course organisers will send full details on application. The Institute has been awarded accreditation by the Council for the Accreditation of Correspondence Colleges.

The advent of formal study courses in boarding kennel management is not only a great help to students but should set a higher standard and ensure a better professional image for small animal boarding establishments nationwide. Although not required by law, formal qualifications are highly desirable and may be influential in certain circumstances – in the case of a dispute, for example.

The boarding cattery

So far, in referring to small animal boarding establishments, those catering for dogs *and* cats have been mentioned. It should be noted that cats are better suited to care in a cattery exclusively for their own kind and there are many such establishments, a few of which come on to the market annually. Occasionally, it may be possible to acquire permission to start a new cattery where a dog boarding kennel would not be allowed. It is essential that a person starting or taking over a cattery has both practical and theoretical training before accepting other people's cats to board.

The fact that cats are in general smaller than dogs, and that most pet cats are neutered so the sex problems of a dog boarding kennel are avoided, are no reasons at all for considering cat boarding as the easier and more lucrative option, and the suggestion is to be deplored. Cats are sensitive, selective and fastidious; close proximity to canine boarders is a great strain on them.

Though cats ideally should be boarded separately from dogs, we do not live in an ideal world. Some pet owners who have both animals prefer to take them to the same boarding kennel, perhaps for personal convenience or possibly because they are not aware of the desirability of separate boarding for each species. It is also more likely that the owner of a dog boarding kennel would be granted permission to add a cattery to his or her business rather than consent being given for a new, exclusive cattery in the same area.

Cats may have considerable difficulty in settling happily into a boarding establishment, more so if they are disturbed by the high noise level of confined dogs; their diet needs careful thought and management, and their health needs constant monitoring despite the fact that all immunisation papers are in order. Cat care can be time-consuming in the extreme; cats are not a get-rich-quick proposition in the boarding context. The knowledge and expertise of the proprietor are most important, and in some cases, less than ideal circumstances are partially outweighed by the high standard of personal care and understanding of cats.

It is because so many boarding kennels accept cats that both dogs and cats are referred to in this book. However, it is strongly advised that people interested in boarding cats, either in a separate cattery or in a mixed kennel should also study the explicit information on boarding kennel construction and management which is published by the Feline Advisory Bureau. The FAB also arranges courses for people who would like to run a cattery, and for young people who wish to work with animals and cats in particular.

Details of FAB publications concerning cattery construction and management, and the training schemes, may be obtained from The Boarding Cattery Officer, Feline Advisory Bureau, 1 Church Close, Orcheston, Nr Salisbury, Wiltshire SP3 4RP.

Taking responsibility for animals

Consider carefully the moral and ethical principles of running your own boarding kennels. You will be assuming the full responsibility for other people's animals, their cherished pets; do you know enough about animals? Loving animals, or thinking you do, and liking a country life are insufficient motives in themselves; they need to be accompanied by training, experience, dedication, discipline and a flair for dealing with people as well as with dogs and cats. The fact that there is no law under which you must prove that you are competent in animal care before you become a boarding kennel owner in no way detracts from the necessity of preparing yourself as much as possible and examining your personal motives as well as your financial resources before you take the plunge. There are many people who think they would like to run boarding kennels; making a success of running your own boarding establishment is more likely to be a long-term proposition than an overnight accomplishment.

Chapter 2

Finding Your Property

It is a natural instinct to start looking at possible properties before considering the finer details of financing. Until you know what is available and have a definite proposition in mind, monetary advice on purchasing is theoretical. However, it is wise to consider how much your maximum investment should be while retaining a certain flexibility of outlook.

Having decided that a boarding kennel is what you want, the next consideration is whether the kennel is to be the sole means of support for you and your family, or whether it is intended to be profitable in its own right but not the only source of family income. A third point needs to be mentioned here: usually kennel properties are sold after the main boarding season, and as every new owner faces the possibility that some alterations will be necessary at the time of takeover, the initial outgoings will race ahead of initial income from the boarding business. Therefore, an additional income may be not only desirable but also necessary at first.

Location

It follows that if either you or your partner must retain present employment, the area in which you conduct your search for a suitable property is restricted. If you are not restricted to a particular area the choice of suitable properties countrywide will show a variation in prices. Land values, the governing factor, are much higher in the home counties and the south-east of England; however, there are thriving boarding businesses in all parts of the British Isles and clients are often prepared to travel many miles to board their pets in a kennel they know and trust. Perhaps you would like a complete change of scenery and look for a business in a part of the country which is completely new to you.

Many kennels are situated on the periphery of urban areas, some deep in the heart of the country. The main considerations are, first, that your kennel is in a position to attract business and second, that it is accessible to your clients.

If the idea of a country property, cut off from civilisation, appeals to you, think whether your clients and friends will be able to find you. The complicated directions such as one sometimes receives, 'A mile past the second pub on the right, down the hill and sharp left between a letterbox and a blasted oak, through the fruit farm and continue' etc, not only is more than many clients can cope with but will certainly have no appeal for drivers of delivery trucks who have had enough of finding impossible places and getting stuck in narrow lanes. Your circle of personal friends might also dwindle but, on the other hand, some thriving businesses exist in such places; perhaps it depends on whether you have a country mind or are ingrained in city ways. A lot may depend on properly signposted directions to the kennel, and if signs have to be posted on land which is not your own, permission has to be obtained: a point on which the District Council should be consulted.

The boarding kennel business which is situated within easy distance of a fair-sized-town, positioned on a well used A or B class road and easily approached despite traffic conditions, is the choice of many. It allows your kennel sign to be on view to passers-by who may remember it when holiday time comes around; it helps you to be found by people unfamiliar with the neighbourhood, and provides easy access for deliveries. Countering an out-of-the-way position with a collection and delivery service for clients not only takes time and petrol but may not suit everybody; pet owners should always see the kennels at which they are boarding their dogs and cats. The kennel tucked away in the country is likely to be a long way from the veterinary surgeon too, and when attention is needed for a boarder it means a visit by the vet, not taking the boarder to the surgery. If you employ staff, accessibility is important for them. In the winter, snow ploughs clear the main roads first; country lanes, particularly those designated as parish by-roads, come last on the council's list. If you find the ideal kennel in a position which might not be a ready-made business location, it is up to you to use your ingenuity to make it a worthwhile business proposition.

Another factor which may help you decide in what area(s) your search for a suitable kennel property might be concentrated is that some areas are already well supplied with small animal boarding establishments and others are short of these facilities. Shortages can be caused by the lack of suitable property or perhaps a rather inflexible attitude towards dog boarding and catteries by an unsympathetic local authority. It may be that there is little business in the area or that hitherto nobody has been prepared to offer such a service, in which case there might be a chance for you. Whatever the area, it is a good plan to check the number of kennels with the Environmental Health Department of the local District Council and to check the dog boarding section of the Yellow Pages which will also cover surrounding areas. In the absence of a national register of boarding kennels it is perhaps fortunate that areas covered by telephone directories are larger than those covered by District Councils, and most boarding kennels advertise in the Yellow Pages.

In boarding establishments everything seems to happen at once! The busiest season – the summer months – coincides with the grass growing rapidly and the weeds flourishing. The property which looks unkempt is unattractive to clients, who are impressed by pleasantly situated properties; unless you are also a dedicated horticulturist, easy landscape upkeep is a priority.

Boarding capacity

Another important question is whether or not you are sure how many boarders you can handle, and how much boarding accommodation is needed for the concern to be profitable as a sole business interest. It is generally accepted that a husband and wife, or two business partners, would have plenty to occupy them in a kennel with a boarding capacity of 50 dogs and maybe 15 to 20 cats if they intended to do all the work themselves. Such work includes, of course, all the general maintenance as well as the care of the animals, and kennels which, from preference or lack of demand, do not board cats may have a higher dog boarding capacity.

People wishing to specialise in a boarding cattery will find that approximately 45 cats are sufficient for a couple to handle without outside assistance. Immediately staff is employed wages become a consideration and many kennels find that part-time help at the busiest times is all they require. Certainly, new boarding kennel owners need to think very carefully about the number of boarders to which they can give the very best care, as some dogs and cats may require far more attention than others and the kennel owner should know each animal individually. However, only at the height of the boarding season are all the kennels likely to be occupied.

Quarantine kennels

There is another class of kennel purchaser: the person who wishes to buy a quarantine kennel. While many of the previously mentioned considerations apply to quarantine kennels, they are international businesses and are usually sought by people with considerable experience of dogs, staff management and business organisation. Quarantine kennel businesses are referred to more fully in Chapter 12.

Starting a new business

One more fact to note before you begin your search for a property is that it may be easier to buy a licensed boarding kennel than to start from scratch at a property you already own, or one on which you already have your eye as an ideal place for a kennel business. The operative word is 'business'. Whether you intend eventually to have a large business with many kennel blocks, or a relatively small boarding concern which is not even intended to provide the sole family income, your kennel *is* a business and you will need a change of use permit to operate at a property which has hitherto been wholly domestic, or which may be a smallholding with either agricultural or horticultural leanings. Boarding kennels do not come under the heading of either agricultural or horticultural pursuits just because the majority of them are situated in rural or semi-rural areas.

Planning permission is needed from the local authority before a change from domestic to business use is possible. It is not only the Planning Department of the District Council which has a say in this matter. The Environmental Health Department may make recommendations, and the local Parish Council is perhaps the most important body in some ways as its opinion, voiced to the District Council Planning Committee Meeting, may be the deciding factor for or against.

The Parish Council and the Environmental Health Officer bear the brunt of neighbourhood complaints about noise. If a new licence to board dogs is granted it may be conditional in the first instance. Too many complaints, and it might not be renewed after a period of three years, in which case it could be impossible to sell the property as a boarding kennel should the owners decide to move. Sometimes, but not always, it is easier to obtain permission for a cattery as the noise problem is minimal, but again, do not bank on sanction from the Parish Council. Reasons such as the alleged spoiling of an area of outstanding natural beauty, increase in traffic and the change of use not being necessary for horticultural or agricultural reasons could be put forward against your proposal.

If you are determined to start from scratch, contact the local Planning Department first to assess what chance of success you might have. Second, consult the Chief Environmental Health Officer of the district for an opinion on whether your present property, or one you are considering, might be thought suitable for small animal boarding purposes, and third, do *not* buy a property without written proof that planning consent would be granted. It would be easier to start with a licensed property, even if it were far removed from your ideal, and concentrate on improving it to the standard you require. It is not impossible in every case to obtain permission to start a new boarding kennel business from what was originally a domestic residence, but the difficulties are considerable. Local authorities are more likely to look kindly on a request for permission to enlarge a small licensed kennel, provided the need can be shown, than to allow another new business in the area.

Buying an existing business

With a fair idea of the size and type of kennel property you require, and remembering to be flexible, what next? See as many properties as possible, which will be time-consuming and may involve many miles of travelling. The major agencies handling sales of kennel properties advertise regularly in the weekly papers *Our Dogs* and *Dog World*, and in the monthly magazine *Kennel and Cattery Management* (see Appendix for addresses). Local estate agents also handle kennel properties occasionally. You may also consider placing an advertisement in the classified section of *Our Dogs* and *Dog World* stating that you are seeking a kennel property.

Having received details of properties which you would like to view, check that they are still available before making a long journey. A telephone call in advance could also reassure you that you really want to see the property, or ascertain that it has some drawback which would be too difficult for you to overcome. In comparison with other businesses, there are relatively few licensed kennels offered for sale at any one time; look not only at the present situation but at future possibilities. Make a list of your essentials and realise that no property will have everything right.

On arriving in the area, pop into a local shop (there is usually a general store in most villages) and ask the shopkeeper if there are any good boarding kennels for dogs and cats in the area. The reply could provide you with vital information.

When you start viewing kennel properties what should you look for?.

Smell

The first thing you may notice about any property you visit is either the smell, or the fact that there is no unpleasant odour about the place. Kennels do not have to smell awful; good husbandry and proper disinfection will keep the property sweet and clean despite the fact that animals are not toilet trained. A property which stinks is one to cross off your list as the basic hygiene is obviously lacking, and if accumulations of filth have been allowed to seep into unsealed wood or concrete what other unhygienic practices are there? Could you ever rid the place of the smell, possible infection, a flea population and more bugs than you ever imagined existed? Your nose will tell you a lot, but so will the general condition of the kennels. Are they really clean? Is there any mess lying around? Uneaten food? Such things attract rats, and do you want to be offering cosy boarding accommodation to all the local rodent population?

Construction

What sort of kennel construction has been used? Are the kennels purpose built or converted from other buildings? Are they built of wood, brick or breeze block. Not all district councils will allow wooden buildings for dog boarding although they may be acceptable for catteries. Are the kennels inside with no attached runs? The recommendations are that each kennel should have its own attached run to which the dog should have free access. Are there additional fenced exercise areas where the dogs can run free several times a day? Are there safety corridors, particularly in a cattery? Is there a good secure perimeter fence to the whole property? You cannot afford escapes; some dogs can jump 6 feet with ease. Is the perimeter fence a 'jackal' fence, that is with a top section inclined inwards to the property? Is the accommodation geared to large, powerful breeds or suited only to smaller breeds? Is there a grassed exercise area? This is a necessity as some pet dogs will only urinate on grass. Are there any covered runs? A boon in wet weather! Bear in mind there is more than one way of setting up a workable kennel.

Is there good storage for foodstuffs, equipment and cleaning accessories? What about the boarders' food preparation area? Is the dog kitchen clean and conveniently placed?

The boarders

Look at the boarders themselves. Are they happy? They will bark at you, but note if they look cheerful. If they do not bark but just sit on their beds, consider whether they have been tranquillised! Why? Can the present boarding kennel owner not tolerate the noise, or have the neighbours complained? Find out. It is most undesirable to tranquillise dogs unless there is a medical reason for it. Are the dogs clean, skinny, bright eyed, fat? What is your general impression? No, you are not conducting a medical examination but trying to get an idea of the care which has been given, and possibly the reputation of the business. At night are the kennels the sort which may make the dogs feel as if they have been shut in a cupboard and forgotten, or can they see other dogs across an aisle? Remember you will be boarding pets used to living in human-sized accommodation; subjecting them to confinement in a kennel which would make a good coal bunker is not going to keep them happy and well. Pet dogs are used to their human family connections; they are also pack animals if left to their own devices; they are not loners as a rule and like to be aware of the presence of companions.

Cat accommodation

Check any cat accommodation carefully. The idea that as cats are small they need minimal room is erroneous. The ideal accommodation is a single chalet for each cat, approximate measurements 4 × 4 × 6 feet in height and with an attached run entered from a safety corridor. Chalets should be separate buildings or, if they are adjacent, a perspex sneeze barrier may be required between each run. Cat accommodation in a mixed species kennel should be out of sight of the dogs though it will be impossible in such circumstances to site a cattery out of earshot of dogs.

Indoor catteries may be of a 'corridor kennel' type, and each cat's compartment should be no less than 5 × 4 × 6 feet and lead to an outside run. It is unfortunate that people do not realise that small cage accommodation must come as a terrible shock to the average pet cat used to a house, and that many prospective kennel owners may visit numerous establishments without seeing the ideal accommodation and therefore think that what they have seen is right.

Heating

Are the heating arrangements in both dog kennels and cat units animal proof, efficient and safe? Economy comes lower down the list than safety, but individual heating for each boarder means an overall economy when a kennel is not full, which is usually in the winter. Heating arrangements which give off fumes are best avoided for reasons of safety and efficiency, and night storage heating is unsatisfactory in a kennel. Heating arrangements can be altered, or if non-existent can be installed to your requirements; allow for the expense. Note whether there are thermostatic controls on present heating arrangements as these are both economical and a great asset to the animals' comfort and wellbeing.

Drainage

When viewing a kennel, ask about the drainage system and the disposal of kennel rubbish. Is the dwelling house on main drainage, septic tank or cesspool drainage? Cesspools need regular emptying. Does the kennel have its own septic tank? Is the disposal of kennel soil by incineration? Is there a purpose-made incinerator? Find out. Also, never be misled by anyone who claims that a septic tank drainage system never needs maintenance. Many tanks were installed before the advent of detergents which interfere with the bacterial breakdown of the contents; modern septic tanks are usually larger than older ones which were not planned to cope with extra loads of water from automatic washing machines. Blockages sometimes occur. The council will empty tanks – for a fee – and a builder may be needed to trace and rectify a blockage. This may sound like an insurmountable problem to a town dweller who takes main drainage for granted, but country folk soon come to grips with such problems. Rural drainage systems are quite satisfactory provided you know something about the way they work and where to go for help. Anyway, you do not pay rates on septic tanks, which theoretically do not need emptying but should be periodically checked, and the council reduces its charges for regular attention. Septic tanks and cesspools may also be emptied by private contractors. For information, consult the Yellow Pages under the heading 'Sewage Consultants'.

Boarding fees and licences

Also enquire about the boarding fees currently charged. These may vary from one part of the country to another, reflecting the general local costs. However, food costs, fuel charges and mortgage rates do not alter from one region to another. It is useful to know what other kennels charge in the same area. Refer to the Yellow Pages

– the local library will have copies of telephone directories – and make a few phone calls; these will provide you with the answers both to average local boarding fees and whether or not the kennels have vacancies.

Boarding licence

Find out the boarding licence renewal fee. These fees are set at the discretion of the District Council and in rural areas are generally quite reasonable. The fees are reviewed every year and are known to be higher in more urban areas. The licence is issued to the owner, not to the property; therefore, when you have found a property which you like, check with the local authority that there is no reason for a licence to be refused to a new owner, provided he or she fulfils the only personal requirement needed, namely no conviction for cruelty to animals or being banned from keeping them. Very occasionally, and for various reasons, when a boarding kennel is offered for sale the local authority may decide that the property should not be used again as a small animal boarding establishment; one reason may be that the licence was conditional in the first place and there were too many complaints from neighbours.

What is a neighbour? If you have always lived in a built-up area you probably consider as your neighbours those who live next door, or whose gardens adjoin your own. In a rural situation your neighbours may be quite a way from you, out of sight in fact. You may even think of a place as isolated because you cannot see another house. Unfortunately, noise carries even greater distances when barking is not masked by other background noises or absorbed by bricks and mortar; you may find a host of neighbours appearing from nowhere, or so it may seem.

Owner's accommodation

Naturally, it is important that the dwelling house suits your needs. Many people searching for a boarding kennel property find that if the kennels are right the house is wrong, or vice versa. Sometimes compromises can be made, and once in a while everything will be right. The priorities for the owner's accommodation are largely decided by the individual's needs, but the house should at least be tolerable as it stands because your energy will be directed to establishing your kennel business, and domestic considerations may have to take second place. Some people cannot turn a blind eye to a decor which does not suit their tastes or be happy in what they consider uncomfortable surroundings, and it is important to realise that as your kennel business will be demanding you need to be able to relax in your home and not be depressed by it.

The location of the dwelling house in relation to the kennel buildings is something you should consider. There are boarding kennels which have the owner's accommodation very close to the dogs' quarters, and some where it is well separated. In the first instance you will have some kennels which will be handy in bad weather or for dogs needing special attention; such kennels may also be a confidence booster for the small pet which has never been away from home before and is feeling forlorn. There will also be barking in close proximity, and though this may be irritating in one way it is often a warning that something is amiss or that visitors are arriving. You soon learn to distinguish the barking for fun from the excited 'Here comes dinner' chorus and the 'What's happening now?' canine voice.

Where the kennel buildings are well separated from the owner's house it may be quieter, but there may be some very wet, cold and dark journeys to check the kennels late at night. In such kennel layouts, ensure that there is adequate outside lighting and that all kennel buildings are secure from intruders. There have been thefts of dogs from boarding kennels, and there are, unfortunately, dangers from people who either do not share our love of animals or misguidedly feel they are being ill-treated. It may be possible to install some form of alarm system – perhaps even an adaptation of a baby alarm – to alert the owner in case of need. The most sophisticated arrangement is closed circuit television, but that is not yet in evidence in many kennels.

Financial enquiries

When you have found a boarding kennel business in which you are seriously interested and intend to go forward with financial enquiries of your own, you will need to see the kennel's audited accounts, if they exist! Sometimes kennels, particularly those which have been considered by their owners more as a paying hobby than a fully-fledged business, have no detailed accounts. A great deal of the trade will probably have been on a cash basis and the turnover nowhere near the VAT bracket. There is often a tendency to keep a kennel ticking over gently as owners cut down their work-load for one reason or another because the kennel is also their home. In such cases look at the business potential; if you can acquire such a property for a reasonable price and build it up again businesswise, you may have a bargain. Financial matters are discussed in more detail in Chapter 4.

Chapter 3

Professional and Other Advice

Although the boarding kennel owner's business is the care and wellbeing of other people's pet animals, it is equally important that basic business practices are understood, as profitability is necessary for the owner to be able to give the service intended. There seems to be an unfortunate element in society which intimates that it is not quite acceptable to make money out of boarding pet animals, but the boarding kennel owner is providing a valuable service and deserves to have a reasonable standard of living and a good professional image.

Property

The prospective owner who is buying a kennel which already has a licence will probably need to borrow money to complete the purchase and is likely to run into the first problem when it is found that his purchase falls into two categories: a dwelling house and a business plus land. A mortgage may be available on the dwelling house but not on the business and therefore financial help will have to be procured from another source. Money must also be available to keep the kennel in operation from the time of the takeover, as foodstuffs will have to be bought in advance and clients do not pay their dogs' hotel bills until they collect them. Obviously, no dog departs from your kennel until its holiday has been paid for! In many cases a deposit or booking fee is payable in advance and this is not returnable in case of cancellation, but advance booking fees are not enough to keep the kennel running and suppliers of animal foods usually prefer to work on a cash with order or cash on delivery basis.

The potential kennel owner who already owns a house, has been granted a permit for a change of use from domestic to business purposes, and intends to build boarding kennels there, having obtained planning permission too of course, may also need financial assistance. Apart from the actual building of the kennels, the initial running costs will have to be covered. Every case is highly individual and advice needs to be tailored to a particular situation. Building societies are, as a rule, interested in private house purchases rather than business property though, especially if you have been saving with one, it is worth asking them for a loan.

Raising finance

The cheapest money with which to finance a new business is your own – personal savings, realisable assets such as jewellery and antiques; if you need to borrow, obtain only what you need and when you need it.

Loans

Private loans from friends or relatives may take the form of their guaranteeing a bank overdraft, or a formal loan, the terms of which should be drawn up by a solicitor. It should be made clear that such a loan does not include any control of the business.

Banks need to establish that you are a good risk before they will lend you money for a business; the manager will need to see a business plan which shows the estimated setting-up costs, the overheads or fixed costs, and the variable costs.

The setting-up costs cover professional fees, the property and initial equipment purchases, initial repairs and decoration. The fixed costs are those which you pay whether business is coming in or not: rent or mortgage repayment, rates, interest charges, HP, telephone, power, insurance, running a car, and paying yourself a salary. The variable, or running, costs include pets' food, vets' bills (if not covered by insurance) and wages to staff. To pay the overheads and running costs, you need working capital, so you should not use all your own money on setting up; lenders are more willing to invest in tangible assets.

The Government Loan Guarantee Scheme guarantees 70 per cent of a loan made by a bank up to a loan limit of £100,000 when the business proposition is basically sound but the borrower cannot put up enough money. A premium of 2½ per cent of the amount outstanding quarterly in advance is payable to the government. Additionally, an interest rating of not less than 2½ per cent over the bank's base rate is payable to the bank for this privilege, so it is not exactly cheap money.

Your business plan, which will help to crystallise your own thoughts as well as persuade the bank to lend you money, should include:

- Name and address of proposed proprietor.
- Details of proposed business venture and its location.
- Information about the proprietor(s); a curriculum vitae with evidence of your ability to run the business.
- Premises. Full information, including present use, and whether planning permission is necessary for your business.
- The market research you have done on the demand for such a business in the area.
- Your financial requirements for the setting up, showing how much money is coming from which sources.
- Information on the services you plan to offer at the start and after a year.
- Staff. Whether your partner or the family will suffice, or what staff you will need to employ (full or part time).
- Budgeted expenses for the first and second years.
- Cash flow forecast for the budget periods.
- Personal and financial references.

Take detailed schedules along with you to show the bank manager when you make an appointment with him.

Business structure

However you start your business, you must decide whether you intend to be a sole trader, to form a partnership or to trade as a limited company.

As a *sole trader* you will be entering the simplest form of business management and, apart from disclosing information connected with ownership of the business as required in the Companies Act 1985 if you are trading under a name other than your own, there are no other formalities. The Inland Revenue and the Department of Social Security should be informed as soon as you start trading. You become self-employed, and are liable for all the debts but collect all the profits.

A *partnership* has two or more proprietors. All may share any profits, and each partner is equally responsible for all the firm's debts. A properly drawn up partnership agreement is essential for, should things go wrong, as they often do, it can be extremely difficult to settle affairs. Many partnerships go wrong because disputes and disagreements which occur had not been allowed for when setting up the partnership. Never enter into any agreement with a short-time acquaintance; never sign anything except a formal deed of partnership drawn up by a solicitor.

Often it is a tragedy which brings disaster to a partnership, such as the death of a partner, or a partner or partners' divorce proceedings; such events may terminate a business enterprise too. Tax assessments are issued in the name of the partnership, but if one partner fails to pay his or her share of the liability the others have to pay it all. Partnerships can work, but they can also be the source of many problems.

Sole traders and partnerships pay Schedule D tax: income from trades, professions or vocations. They can set against profits legitimate business expenses such as the running costs of the business, wages and salaries paid to employees, insurance, some legal and professional fees, and the cost of goods bought for resale.

A *limited company* is a legal entity in its own right, and few kennel owners operate in this way.

Whether you buy a company 'off the shelf' from a registration agent or set up one yourself, professional advice from a solicitor is essential. The objects of the company are set out in the Memorandum and Articles of Association. Limited companies are obliged by law to keep accounts to a prescribed formula, have them audited, and submit a set annually to Companies House. On small business corporation tax is levied at 25 per cent on profits under £250,000 and 35 per cent on profits between £250,000 and £1,250,000 per annum, payable nine months from the end of the accounting period. The period over which trading losses can be carried back and set against profits has been extended from one to three years. Business expenses that can be claimed against profits are similar to those for sole traders and partnerships.

Free advice

England and Wales

Training and Enterprise Councils (TECS) are being established in England and Wales. One of their priorities is to improve the network of services for smaller businesses and provide easy access to specialist business advice. They should be particularly useful as TEC advisers will have specialist knowledge relevant to the areas they serve.

As prospective boarding kennel owners may be considering starting their business, or taking over an existing business, in another part of the country, contacting the TEC in their own area is the first step. The address and telephone number may be obtained from the local Job Centre, or from Directory Enquiries if it is not shown in the current telephone book.

The local Training and Enterprise Council may provide initial counselling, but will also be able to give you details of the TEC serving the area in which your prospective business is situated and which will have information regarding business prospects in that area. TEC services are free of charge and relate to matters concerning all the aspects which apply to businesses in general and your counsellor will be an experienced businessman. Though possibly never having set foot in a boarding kennel his or her expert business advice may help you to start your boarding kennels. The physical care of your boarders is covered by this book.

The Rural Development Commission, which operates in England only, may also be of help to intending boarding kennel owners, though the Commission's prime function is to help your business to grow and prosper. The RDC may be contacted at 141 Castle Street, Salisbury, Wiltshire SP1 3TP, telephone 01722 336245, and you will be put in touch with a counsellor in your area.

Scotland
If you are considering setting up or purchasing an existing boarding kennel in Scotland, the Scottish Business Shop, telephone 0141-248 6014, should be able to provide you with the advice you need, or direct you to a local office in the aea in which your prospective business is situated.

Northern Ireland
In Northern Ireland, the Local Enterprise Development Unit (LEDU), telephone 01232 242582, offers advice and counselling on small businesses. The Northern Ireland Training Authority, telephone 01232 365171, may also provide you with information.

Readers should note that boarding kennels do not come under the auspices or jurisdiction of The Kennel Club which has an entirely different role in the world of dogs.

Solicitor

Your solicitor is probably the person to give you the most important advice of all. No purchase of property should be attempted without a legal consultation, and no partnership entered into without a legal agreement drawn up by your solicitor. No papers should be signed without careful reading on your part, and all ordnance survey maps of the property should be checked to see that the boundaries shown are correct.

When you have decided on a property and have investigated the financial details, and have been reassured by the District Council in writing that the boarding licence will be re-issued in your name, your solicitor will handle the legal matters and make the necessary land searches. As most kennels are situated in rural or semi-rural areas your solicitor should check whether permission has been granted, or application made, for any change of use of adjoining land though it be agricultural at the present time. The construction of new roads, a bypass or motorway for example, may be beneficial in the long run. However, should a neighbouring farmer have been granted permission to site an intensive pig or poultry rearing unit in a field adjoining your kennel or cattery, it may be a distinct disadvantage to you. In the case of future applications you should receive notification, on which you may take action; should you not be aware that permission has already been granted your position may be threatened. Rural areas are not always as passive as they seem at first sight and some agricultural pursuits can be smelly and noisy, and attract flies and rodents which would spread to your property.

A major problem which has affected some established boarding kennels in recent years is the encroachment by new property developments on what was previously open country, thus bringing human habitation closer to the kennels. New residents tend to complain about noise, justifiable or not, and you may find yourself in need of legal advice. Of course you should do your best to keep aware of proposed new housing developments, which are usually a prominent subject in local newspapers, and it could be to your advantage to grasp the nettle and suggest to the developers that they may like to mention your excellent services in their promotional literature which describes the amenities of the area.

The cost of professional advice could be far less than any costs incurred through not taking it, and as noted above, a great deal of professional advice may actually be free!

Insurance

You will need professional advice on insurance. Apart from the obvious fire, theft, storm damage and accidental injury policies, kennels need insurance which covers the owner and staff, and the boarders while they are in the kennels or in transit between home and kennels. There should be insurance against escape from your premises, reimbursement of fees for you in certain cases, and payment of veterinary fees incurred while the animal is in your care. There is no greater misery than a client finding his pet has escaped and been lost, or has been stolen from your kennels; reimbursement from the insurance company may help. Your business suffers a setback when a client returns to find an ailing dog and a vet's bill a mile long.

It is not enough for an owner to agree that, should veterinary care be needed for the pet while it is in your kennel, you are empowered to call a veterinary surgeon to visit the animal. The vet's bill has to be paid, and bearing in mind the fact that many illnesses occur in what are generally termed unsocial hours, or at weekends, bank holidays and such times, and that the vet must visit the kennels, the fees are sure to be considerable. If, on the other hand, health problems have arisen with a boarder but you can meet your client with the news that the pet has been treated and that your insurance has covered the cost of treatment, or that compensation is payable in some circumstances, though it cannot prevent some sorrow it can obviate hard feelings.

Pet Plan Insurance Ltd and Dog Breeders Insurance Co Ltd both specialise in boarding kennel insurance. Contact these firms and consult their representatives for an expert assessment of your own particular situation. You will find that for a relatively small sum per day, which could be added to your boarding fees without making them exorbitant, your boarders can be completely covered by insurance and you are freed from any worries in this respect. Proper insurance not only protects the dogs and their owners, it also protects your reputation.

In a physically demanding business, accidental injury is more than a remote possibility. You should consider that, if you were even temporarily disabled, it might be necessary to pay someone to do your work. Insurance coverage can help in such situations. If your staff are self-employed or casual workers it would be wise to talk to them about personal accident insurance too.

In the kennel business there are a few grey areas on which it is impossible to give definitive advice. Insurance against being sued is also worth discussion.

You may wish to consult an insurance broker. The British Insurance and Investment Brokers Association, telephone 0171-623 9043, can send you a list of insurance brokers in your area.

Accounting

You may already have an accountant. If not, or perhaps because you are moving into an entirely new area, you may wish to ask for advice on accountancy firms from a local bank manager. Your accountant will advise you what *he* requires. It will be necessary to keep careful accounts, though you may have found during your search for a boarding kennel that many owners could not produce audited accounts, or that some accounts which were produced were incomprehensible. Kennels are indeed busy places in which the boarders come first and everything else takes second place; when the day's physical work is done it is too easy to put off the bookwork. That is not the road to profitability.

Local officials

It would be advisable to contact the Chief Environmental Health Officer of the local District Council and discuss with him any matters concerning the continued approval of the kennel as a boarding establishment, or the possibility of enlarging it. Each District Council has its own recommendations on boarding kennels and its Environmental Health Department approves the site, the buildings, the drainage and waste disposal with a view to health matters and noise pollution. Complaints of undue noise, or any noise at all in some instances, are made to the Environmental Health Officer who will investigate them. In contrast, council officials are probably not aware of the best ways to handle your boarders' day-to-day needs; they are concerned with the suitability of the property from their point of view, not necessarily from yours. Neither is the council interested in your personal suitability, training, or experience with animals other than the fact that you have not been convicted for cruelty to animals.

Complaints of cruelty, or alleged cruelty, are made to the RSPCA and it is useful to contact your local RSPCA inspector in your early days of kennel ownership as you may be asked to assist this organisation at times by temporarily housing a dog or cat. While you should be aware that the RSPCA do not have an automatic right of entry to your property, and would have to produce a police warrant to gain admittance against your wishes, it is wise to build a good rapport with them and to instil confidence in your ability and business.

As kennel owners are always advised to insist that all boarders should have current immunisation certificates, it therefore does not make sense to accept a rescued animal which has no health records. If you have no accommodation for such animals you must make it clear that you cannot accept them. Even if your kennel has a separate isolation unit which could be used in such circumstances, you are not obliged by law to take in such animals with their possible health risks, and your paying clients do not deserve to have their pets endangered. It is best to discuss such matters fully with your local police and RSPCA so that they are aware of your decision and whether or not you can help in exceptional circumstances. These organisations are fellow professionals and you all deserve to know the policies and not be forced into last-minute decisions which may be based solely on emotive reasons. The difference between you and these other bodies is that you are self-employed and cannot afford to take risks which might be detrimental to your business, while they are funded.

Police dogs, that is, those owned by the force and not strays, are another matter. Occasionally accommodation is needed for these dogs, which are healthy and fully inoculated. This is a different matter entirely and subject to special negotiation.

When you take over another person's business the ideal arrangement is to take over the kennels empty and arrange for a thorough cleaning and disinfection before your customers arrive. In practice this may not work and you may find yourself taking over a kennel in mid-season or with some boarders in residence even though the summer rush is over. You will undoubtedly be glad of their boarding fees anyway, but it would be a good plan to rotate the accommodation so that you can have a thorough cleansing and disinfecting job done by a specialist professional firm. Your residents can then be changed over to the professionally disinfected buildings while the others are being treated. A cleaning and disinfecting routine as suggested by the professional organisation should ease your worries concerning proper disease control on your premises. Waiting until you have an outbreak of disease is leaving it too late.

The Ministry of Agriculture, Fisheries and Food, or MAFF as you will come to know this government department, may also be consulted either at their head office or through the local Divisional Veterinary Officer at a MAFF area office. The area address will be found in the telephone directory, and the head office address is shown on page 138.

Chapter 4
Finance and Running Costs

The estimation of running costs for a boarding kennel business during the first year of ownership is not an easy task. Hopefully, you will have seen your predecessor's audited accounts, but even so your running costs may bear no relation to those. In the first place, all costs are sure to have risen, and second, your priorities may not have been the same as those of the previous owner. The other, perhaps the most important, factor is that you do not know how much business you will be doing. Perhaps your predecessor has allowed the business to lapse, and while you may have been able to purchase it at an advantageous price, estimating how much and how soon you can build it up may be impossible to forecast with any accuracy.

Income

Boarders' fees will probably provide most of your income when you start up. Reckon on being full a third of the year and allow, say, £6.00 per day per medium-sized dog (without VAT). When you multiply your kennels by £2.00 and then by 365, it will give you the worst picture. Any other sales of goods or accommodation will bring in more. It is clear that an additional income from outside the business is often essential during the early stages.

If a married couple is running the business together, the wife could be paid the equivalent of the personal allowance before paying income tax, which is £4045 a year at present (1997–8).

Outgoings

Some expenses will be the same whether you are doing business or not. Rent, mortgage or loan repayments can be estimated with fair accuracy, barring fluctuations in interest rates, and can be paid monthly. Many bills – gas, electricity, telephone and some water authority charges – may be also paid on a monthly basis. This can ease the shock of a sheaf of bills arriving at the same time, and in the case of varying accounts such as electricity, gas and telephone you will receive statements which will show you how your payments are matching up with your debts. Heating and lighting charges can be estimated by the Boards concerned, and may or may not work out exactly at the end of the year.

The licence renewal fee must be thought of, but these fees are reviewed each year and vary in different parts of the country. There may be some extra expense for the periodic drainage of septic tanks, but the local council or sewerage disposal service usually has a set rate for this and reduces the charge for regular attention. However, any unblocking must be contracted for separately with a private contractor; allow for this.

Depending on what disposal system you have at your kennel, and what refuse collecting services are offered by the local council under your general rates, you may find that you have to pay extra for the collection of garbage which may come under the heading of trade waste rather than domestic refuse. Question this in advance for, as in the case of a non-functioning septic tank, a kennel waste problem needs sorting out immediately, not tomorrow or next week. If this is a situation you have to deal with on an extra payment basis, allow for it, as it will be a continuing problem.

Another expense will be the running costs of your car or van, but make this business item pay its way by using it as an advertising medium – see that it carries the name of your kennels, the location and telephone number, and that it is clean and gives the impression of a hygienic establishment.

Though you may have made some capital investment in additions, alterations and redecoration to the dwelling house and kennels, maintenance and general upkeep of the whole property must be allowed for. Unfortunately the boarders will probably damage their accommodation far more than you would ever have imagined. Kennels and cat units must be escape-proof. Though purpose-made kennels, and kennel gates, runs and fencing may be expensive initially, they are likely to give fewer maintenance problems over the years. Outside exercise runs take a beating too and they, and other grassed parts of the property, will need mowing. Allow for the expense and upkeep of garden machinery and perhaps for some casual labour in this department, as your busiest season will coincide with rapid growth of grass and weeds. Gravel runs may need resurfacing, perhaps not frequently, but it is an expense to bear in mind.

Two further items of major importance are food for the boarders and cleaning materials, including disinfectants. Methods of feeding dogs and cats in the kennel environment are discussed in Chapter 7.

Cleaning materials and disinfectants are another large item in the kennel budget. Chapter 6 deals with disinfectants in some detail; remember that the cheapest are not necessarily the most effective and that disinfection is a vital part of the daily kennel routine.

Stationery and postage costs arise as they will in any business and you should allow for regular local advertising plus occasional advertising farther afield.

You should, of course, remember your own National Insurance obligations. Visit the local offices of the Department of Social Security for advice, remembering that self-employed people (whether kennel owner or staff) with small earnings may obtain exemption from payments as explained in the official leaflet NI 27 A.

Value added tax

VAT is administered by HM Customs and Excise, and your local office will supply the necessary instruction leaflet and show you how to deal with the paperwork. If your annual business turnover exceeds £35,000 (the figure fixed in the 1991 Budget) you must register for VAT, and your accounts will have to show details of all VAT charged to customers (the standard rate is 17.5 per cent). VAT returns have to be completed quarterly, and it is wise to keep VAT collected in a separate bank account, so the cash is available when you have to pay it out and not dipped into for current expenditure. On the credit side, you can claim repayment of VAT on your business purchases: animal foodstuffs, petrol, cleaning materials and so on.

Keeping accounts

When in business on your own account, you should keep the books in a form recommended by your accountant, so he can present them to the Inland Revenue annually for income tax assessment and also prepare a profit and loss account for you. It is easier if the work is done regularly, and it can be very simple.

In the *cash book* will be recorded income (on the left-hand side of a double page spread) and outgoings (on the right-hand side). Each transaction shows on one line the date, description of goods sold or service provided (or bought), cheque number, invoice number, cost, and VAT. The *petty cash book* records small sums paid out daily in cash. The *wages book* – if you employ staff – shows each person's gross earnings, tax deductions,

NI contributions, net pay and the employer's NI contribution as well.

If you deal regularly with certain suppliers, you will find a *purchase ledger* useful, each supplier having a page or section. You are unlikely to have numerous dealings with individual customers, so a *sales ledger* will probably not be called for.

Your accountant should be able to guide you through the maze; the more work you do, the lower the bill will be.

Getting the best deals

The answer to getting the best deals is to approach manufacturers until you find a sympathetic ear! Purpose-built kennels, run fencing, kennel 'furniture and furnishings' – that is, beds and bedding – pet foods and disinfectants are made by firms specialising in products for the pet trade. Many other products, perhaps all, will have to be obtained from general suppliers but not all suppliers are willing to sell to kennels at trade prices. Manufacturers exhibiting at the larger championship dog shows and trade exhibitions are usually helpful.

Meanwhile it remains essential for the kennel owner to ensure that running costs are kept economical through his or her own individual efforts. Always ask for trade prices; you are in business and are buying for your business. Ask for discount on bulk purchases. Check the price of pet foods from several sources – you will be surprised at the variation on individual products. Perhaps there is an agricultural trade supply centre in your area from which you can purchase certain items. When approaching bulk suppliers or cash and carry depots you must have done your homework and know which products you want to buy. These non-kennel orientated merchants will be unable to advise you on products to suit your special needs. The new kennel owner who has experience of dog or cat breeding, exhibiting, nursing or veterinary care has a head start in knowing which are the most useful and advantageous products to buy.

The kennel owner needs to purchase at advantageous prices and cannot afford the time to be constantly chasing after information. This book will give readers some leads from which to work.

Updating your knowledge

In order to make the most of your business potential, it is necessary to regularly update your knowledge of the financial, commercial and animal care aspects of your kennels. Boarding kennels are essentially individual businesses but, unfortunately, that individuality leads to isolation from other businesses in the area, and from others of the same kind.

New, and intending, owners of boarding kennels are strongly advised to read either, or both, of the two weekly dog papers, *Our Dogs* and *Dog World*, which are available to order from your local newsagent, as the features 'Educational Events' and 'Chances To Learn' are published weekly therein and some of the subjects scheduled may be of interest to you.

Courses on various subjects of interest to boarding kennel owners are planned by the College of Animal Welfare, Wood Green Animal Shelters, Godmanchester, Huntingdon PE18 8LJ, telephone 01480 831177. Subjects such as animal first aid, feline behaviour, and kennel and cattery management are among those offered.

It may also be useful to attend some of the lectures which are given occasionally by members of the Association of Pet Behaviour Counsellors. These are always advertised in the weekly canine press and it is well worth making an effort to attend some of them. Money spent on broadening your knowledge is an investment in your business.

Chapter 5

Laws and Orders: Statutory Requirements

Boarding kennel owners should know which laws concern their trade and remember that not all parts of the British Isles, or all types of kennels, are subject to the same laws. However, a law which applies in one country of the United Kingdom will probably have a counterpart which applies in another. One example is the Animal Boarding Establishments Act 1963 which applies to England, Scotland and Wales; the counterparts which apply in Northern Ireland are the Northern Ireland Welfare of Animals Act 1972, and the Animal Boarding Establishments Regulations (NI) 1974.

The Animal Boarding Establishments Act 1963

This requires that dog and cat boarding kennels in England, Scotland and Wales be licensed by the district authority in which they are situated and that they shall be inspected by an officer appointed in writing by that authority. The district authority is required to specify on the licence the conditions which appear to be necessary to secure the objects of the Act. When the Act had been in force for some years it became apparent that boarding kennel conditions varied considerably in different parts of the country; some kennels were decidedly unsatisfactory and there seemed to be no uniform interpretation of the schedule of conditions or the standard of inspection.

In 1970 the British Veterinary Association published a schedule of conditions for the use of local authorities when issuing licences under the Act, but there was still concern in some areas that boarding establishments were not altogether satisfactory. Therefore, in 1975 the BVA published a guide for district authorities and their veterinary inspectors employed under the Act. The guide was revised in 1985 and copies may be obtained for £2.50 from the British Veterinary Association. Telephone 01732 884023 for this publication. This could be the best investment of your entire kennel career! The BVA guide is comprehensive, concise and explicit in describing the conditions under which your kennel should operate.

Apparently excluded from inspection under the 1963 Act are pet shop kennels which are ancillary to the main business as these will be covered by the Pet Animals Act 1951, training kennels for police or guide dogs, obedience training kennels, greyhound kennels and hunt kennels where the hounds belong to the hunt. Breeding kennels are normally covered by the Breeding of Dogs Act 1973, but breeding kennels which are also boarding kennels may be subject to the 1963 Act also. Kennels at airports or hotels, or in other situations where the boarding of animals is not the prime occupation, are also exempt from inspection under the Act. Quarantine kennels are licensed by the Ministry of Agriculture, Fisheries and Food and are inspected under MAFF regulations, not under the 1963 Act, unless they also have domestic boarding sections in which case the 1963 Act will apply to that department as would the Breeding of Dogs Act 1973 should it also be a breeding establishment.

Owners of boarding kennels should obtain a copy of the 1963 Act, not only to become familiar with the conditions which they are expected to fulfil but also to make sure that they understand their own rights. The Act instructs a local authority to pay particular regard to certain requisites before issuing a licence, but without prejudice to their discretion to withhold a licence on other grounds. In short, although a person may be eligible to hold a licence and the premises are apparently suitable to be licensed as a boarding establishment, a licence may be withheld for other reasons. This is particularly important to people who may wish to start a new kennel at a property which seems eminently suitable but for which a licence application may be refused. They are entitled to know why it has been refused or, if a complaint has been made against them, to ask who made the complaint.

Model licence conditions and guidance for dog boarding establishments: A working party report on the Animal Boarding Establishments Act 1963

The above title refers to a report on the work of the Chartered Institute of Environmental Health (CIEH) Animal Boarding Establishments Working Party which was published in 1993, and amended in 1995 following discussions with the British Veterinary Association (BVA), the British Small Animals Veterinary Association (BSAVA), the Feline Advisory Bureau (FAB), the Pet Trade and Industry Association (PTIA) and the Association of District Councils (ADC). This document was prepared in the best interests of animal welfare and to improve kennel management.

Since the implementation of the 1963 Act, the British Veterinary Association published guidance on the licensing of animal boarding establishments in the 1970s and also in the 1980s, comments in the latter document still being relevant. In the past, local authorities were allowed to grant licences to premises which were substandard, provided that they met the required standards by the beginning of 1980. However, it was found that in many cases the required standards were not met, and currently no reason can be seen for issuing licences to any premises which fail to meet the required standards.

Boarding kennel owners, and would-be owners, are strongly recommended to obtain a copy of the Working Party Report as compliance with the recommendations will be necessary for the approval and licensing of your boarding kennel. It is a very comprehensive document and you should also ascertain from your local council whether or not there is a cut-off date by which all of the recommendations in the report must be implemented.

The basic requirements of the Animal Boarding Establishments Act 1963 stipulate that dogs be kept in accommodation of suitable size and construction, temperature, ventilation, lighting and cleanliness. Boarded animals must be adequately supplied with suitable food and drink, and be visited by the kennel staff at suitable intervals. Dogs must be kept in secure accommodation, reasonable precautions are to be taken to prevent the spread of infectious diseases and appropriate steps must be taken in the event of an emergency. A suitable consistent level of management should be maintained.

Kennel inspection

Under the terms of the 1963 Act the district authority may authorise in writing any of its officers, or any veterinary surgeon or veterinary practitioner, to inspect your kennel. You may not obstruct or delay such a person and, in fact, you may come to know your local inspector very well. Despite the wording of the Act the inspector may not be a veterinary surgeon and he is not obliged to have any knowledge of dogs or the animal boarding business; Environment Head Officers, on whom falls most of the work of inspection and investigation of complaints, are not specifically trained in canine and feline knowledge, which is not intended to imply that they have no knowledge of dogs or cats at all.

No person other than the authorised officer of the district authority has any statutory right to inspect your kennels; no representative of any organisation, charitable or otherwise, has a right of entry to your property without your permission. Animal welfare societies do not have an automatic right of entry but, of course, you may invite whom you wish to see your kennels. Make sure that you, and your staff, know who must be admitted and who should await the owner's permission to enter. There is no need to be rude or unwelcoming but, apart from the official inspector, visitors come by appointment. It is important to remember that some people may have visited other boarding establishments prior to yours and that such premises may be neither as clean nor as free from infection as your property and that you have the health of your boarders to consider. Some visitors may be quite content with a talk in your reception area; you should ascertain the purpose of their visit before deciding to show them round the premises. Visitors will be an excitement for your boarders and the dogs will enjoy a good bark. You may prefer that they are not disturbed unnecessarily.

Model licence conditions and guidance for cat boarding establishments: A working party report on the Animal Boarding Establishments Act 1963

The above heading is the title of the relevant CIEH report referring to the boarding conditions and care of cats in such establishments, and is equally as explicit and informative as its sister document which refers to dogs. It is advisable to obtain a copy of both documents from your District Council whether or not you board, or are hoping to board, both species. When new kennels and/or catteries are built, it is expected that they will meet the approved standards, though it is accepted that in existing establishments upgrading may need to be phased in gradually by agreement with the local authority. Whether you are hoping to purchase an existing boarding kennel/cattery business, or whether you are interested in quarantine accommodation, your first step should be to request copies of the CIEH Working Party Reports from the Environmental Health Department of your local council.

The Diseases of Animals (Approved Disinfectants) Order 1978 (amended 1991)

This applies to quarantine kennels which are required to use an approved disinfectant shown on the list included in the Order. However, every boarding kennel owner should have a current copy of the list, which may be obtained from the Ministry of Agriculture, Fisheries and Food, Animal Health Division A, Hook Rise South, Tolworth, Surbiton, Surrey KT6 7NF, telephone 0181–330 4411.

Copies of the above Acts (but not the list of approved disinfectants) may be obtained from HM Stationery Office. Copies of the Northern Ireland Welfare of Animals Act 1982 and the Animal Boarding Establishments Regulations (NI) 1974 may be obtained from HMSO, 80 Chichester Street, Belfast BT1 4JY. Residents of Northern Ireland wishing to enquire about boarding establishments should contact the Department of Agriculture, Dundonald House, Upper Newtownards Road, Belfast, telephone 01232 650111.

Licensing authorities

There are a few boarding establishments situated on some of the smaller British isles and occasionally one of these may be offered for sale. The Isle of Wight is part of the county of Hampshire but has two district councils with authority to issue boarding kennel licences and inspect boarding establishment premises: Medina and South Wight District Councils.

In the Channel Islands, both Jersey and Guernsey have their own separate governments, and Guernsey's regulations usually extend to the island of Alderney. Neither Jersey nor Guernsey has any government regulations concerning small animal boarding establishments, though there are cruelty to animals acts in force under which their animal protection societies could act if requested. These are the Jersey Society for the Prevention of Cruelty to Animals and the Guernsey SPCA whose work is similar to that of the RSPCA. Current boarding kennel fees in the Channel Islands are at present approximately half those in force in the south-east of England, which merely serves to illustrate how prices and fees vary.

The Isle of Man has its own government, and enquiries concerning boarding kennels may be made to the Animal Health Department, IOM Board of Agriculture and Fisheries, Douglas The Animal Boarding Establishments (Isle of Man) Act 1973 is the relevant Act in force, and animal boarding establishments must be licensed and may be inspected by an officer authorised by the Board of Agriculture and Fisheries.

It is noteworthy that regardless of area and despite government Acts and inspection by officers of the district authorities, there is a great variation in small animal boarding establishments, accommodation and administration. They vary from admirable to abysmally awful. For this reason prospective boarding kennel owners are advised to see as many kennel properties as possible even though they may be viewing establishments outside their chosen price range. Extensive viewing is necessary to see both the best and the worst – how else will you be able to set your own standard of achievement?

Liability for damage

Other Acts of Parliament will apply to boarding kennel owners depending on circumstances and conditions: for example, the Animals Act 1971, which applies in England and Wales only, makes provision for civil liability for damage done by animals, protection of livestock from dogs, and for purposes connected with these matters.

Retail trading

Should a boarding kennel owner decide to expand his or her business by selling dog and cat foods and pet accessories (for which planning permission may be necessary from the local authority if sales become more than an ancillary part of the business) the owner will be subject to the Weights and Measures Act and the Trade Descriptions Acts, and in addition will need to be familiar with the Feeding Stuffs Regulations 1982 which were implemented in July 1984.

The Feeding Stuffs Regulations 1982 are intended to protect the health of pets (*all* pets, not only dogs and cats) and to make it quite clear to pet owners what nature of food they are buying. Regulations concerning other animal foods, for pigs and cows for example, have existed for some time. These regulations affect the boarding kennel owner in two ways – in the food that they buy for their boarders and the food which they sell to their clients if the kennel also has a retail shop. Dog and cat food must display on its packaging the name and description of the food, state what animals it is intended for, give directions for use, state the net weight, show a list of ingredients in descending order by weight, and list certain additives. It is the responsibility of the company or person whose name appears on the pack to ensure that the information is correct; these regulations apply to compound foodstuffs, not 'plain' products such as fish or meat which are not part of a mixed food.

In a kennel shop, and in some pet shops, difficulties arise when some products – for example the particular dry dog food you serve to your boarders and want to offer to your clients when the boarder goes home – are sold loose because you have purchased it in 20 kg sacks but customers wish to buy it by the pound. If a product is sold loose from a bin, bag or box the relevant details concerning the food will have to be displayed. If you prepack products into handy size bags to display on shelves, the law states that it is not necessary to label every bag as long as the details of the product contents are displayed at the point of sale. It would be far better to make sure that pet foods sold loose should be packed in a container which bears a label stating the contents and how to use them. Most pet owners do not sufficiently understand the differences between complete and complementary foods, or that the amounts required by animals of some foods will not be the same as with other products. Solve this problem by dealing with manufacturers who market their products in small packs for pet owners as well as in large sacks for you!

Terms for boarding

The most frequent point of civil law in connection with the boarding kennel business arises from dogs and cats being booked into a boarding establishment and not being collected at the end of their vacation. Most boarding kennel owners state on their booking forms that if animals are not collected within 15 days of their due departure date, and no communication from the owner or the owner's agent is received, and if attempts by the kennel to contact them fail, the kennel reserves the right to dispose of the animals. Though the booking form, which should be signed by the pet owner and the kennel owner, is a contract, it is impossible to state definitely whether the right to dispose clause may be implemented. This is a situation which is most worrying and happens far too frequently. It seems that some irresponsible pet owners choose this method as a soft option to abandon animals they no longer wish to keep. Sometimes boarding kennel owners find they have two or three pets for which no fees have been paid and which are occupying accommodation booked by another client.

Kennel owners should serve notices on pet owners to the effect that they owe a specified amount for the animal's board and that unless the account is settled within a specified time further action will be taken to collect money and dispose of the pet(s). The kennel owner can apply to the magistrates court for advice; it will cost money and still probably not recover the fees. It costs money to have animals destroyed by the veterinary surgeon, and there is the natural reluctance to take such a step anyway. Efforts can certainly be made to re-home them, though if they are sold it will most likely be at a considerable loss. It seems that kennel owners would be well advised to consult their own solicitors because of the complexities of contractual law.

It is too easy to say that such situations should be avoided. When a boarding kennel is well established it might be possible to ask that new clients settle their pets' boarding fees in advance whereas known clients would not be asked to do so. However, new kennel owners will take a year at least to meet their 'regulars', though some information may be gleaned from their predecessor's records. In the course of what is admittedly inconclusive research (because the sample is necessarily a small one) it has been observed that in all cases of the abandonment of pets in boarding kennels the pet owners had housing difficulties. There are, of course, many genuine cases of house moving when it is

BEERODE BOARDING KENNELS

Proprietors: J & M Doe

BEERODE
Nr ANYTOWN
Tel: Beerode 4321

BOOKING APPLICATION FORM

I accept Beerode Boarding Kennels' conditions of boarding as shown in their brochure and wish to board my dog(s)/cats(s)

From: .... To: ....
Owner's name: .... Tel: ....
Address: ....
Temporary address: ....
Address of contact: ....
Dog(s) names: .... Ages(s): ....
Breed or Description: ....
Cats(s) names: .... Ages(s): ....
Breed or Description: ....
Normal foods: ....
Usual veterinary surgeon: ....

NO DOGS/CATS WILL BE ACCEPTED WITHOUT A CURRENT VACCINATION CERTIFICATE

I understand that while every care will be given to my animals they are boarded entirely at my own risk. I authorise you to call a veterinary surgeon on my behalf should it be necessary. I enclose a deposit of £ . . . . which I understand is not returnable if the booking is cancelled and that the boarding fees are due for the full booking should I collect my animals before the due date of departure.

Beerode Boarding Kennels reserve the right to dispose of animals not collected within 15 days of the stated departure date if no communication from the owner, of the owner's agent, is received, and if efforts to contact the owners fail.

Signed: .... Signed: ....
    (Beerode Kennels)   (Owner)

desirable for pets to be boarded during the actual moving operation, and it can be very hard to differentiate between the genuine and the shady story. Similarly, pets often need to be boarded during the owner's hospitalisation, and in such circumstances some owners may be eligible to receive help towards boarding fees from the Social Services. Perhaps after a time every boarding kennel owner develops a sixth sense for these types of people, but almost every kennel gets caught at some time or other.

Certain types of kennels are exempt from inspection under the 1963 Animal Boarding Establishments Act. Some of these apparently exempt kennels may, in some ways, threaten a boarding kennel owner's business, but more direct threats appear from unlicensed quarters. The services offered by individuals who advertise pet walking/visiting services in the pet owner's absence are outside the jurisdiction of the 1963 Act and consist of visits to the house to feed and exercise the pets which, apart from the visits, are left to their own devices. Organisations providing personnel to live in the home with the animal during an owner's absence are also outside the jurisdiction of the 1963 Act.

Chapter 6

Health Matters

Kennel owners need to be experts in cleaning and hygiene, and in training their staff to carry out these duties daily. Anything less than perfection in these tasks creates a foothold for the development of health problems. Kennel cleaning, unless properly understood and carried out, may have hazards of its own. The proper cleaning of kennels inevitably requires the use of chemicals, some of which may come under COSHH (Control of Substances Hazardous to Health) regulations and care must be exercised in their storage and use.

Always read the labels, and store and use cleaning chemicals strictly according to directions. It is strongly advised that you purchase your kennel cleaning requirements from a company which specialises in chemicals formulated for use in the boarding kennel and the veterinary profession, as such companies are always available for advice if required. Your own veterinary surgeon should be able to recommend a suitable company. Keep a check on cleaning materials and re-order before stocks become too low. Do not hesitate to enquire from the manufacturers whether cleaning chemicals have any carcinogenic qualities, and if they do, choose another product if appropriate.

It should not be assumed that kennel assistants automatically know of the benefits, and hazards, of the cleaning and disinfecting agents they will be required to use, so they must be properly trained in their use and should, of course, be provided with protective clothing. Overalls, rubber gloves and wellington boots are basic essentials and protective eye glasses (plastic ones which can actually be worn over normal spectacles if necessary) are also a necessity. Just one small splash in the eye of any irritant from dish washing detergent to kennel disinfectant can be both extremely painful and dangerous. Should that type of accident occur seek medical advice immediately. Kennel assistants must take cleaning chores seriously for the sake of their own health and safety as well as that of the boarded animals.

Kennel cleaning

Cleaning is a daily routine, a procedure which must be thorough despite any temptation to skimp the job. This has to be impressed very firmly on new staff. The microscopic organisms which have caused serious setbacks to many kennels, and been the downfall of some, are always present. Micro-organisms can even thrive and multiply in such places as around chips in enamel feeding bowls or on the frayed edges of chewed and battered plastic dishes, quite apart from the obvious corners. Proper daily cleaning plus regular super cleaning of kennels between one boarder leaving and the next taking up residence; the periodic 'spring clean', usually undertaken in the slack season or perhaps when one kennel block is not in use – all will help to keep micro-organisms (bacteria and viruses) at bay.

Tools and equipment

For the cleaning operations, brooms, brushes, dustpans and 'pooper-scoopers' are indispensable, and a vacuum cleaner with a long extension hose will remove dust which accumulates on high ledges. Buckets and mops, and stiff 'yard' brooms are other essentials and all these items should be heavy duty as they will take a lot of wear and tear. Each kennel block should have its own set of cleaning tools; in the case of disease breaking out in one block, the less interchange of equipment between blocks the better. Specialist equipment such as pooper-scoopers can be purchased from kennel suppliers whose advertisements will be found in the weekly dog papers, or may be available at dog shows or from some pet accessory suppliers. Kennel vacuum cleaners are probably those which have been displaced by fancier models in the house or purchased second-hand, the cylinder or industrial type being the most useful. Mops, deck scrubbing brushes, brooms and buckets should all be chosen for ease of use as well as durability, or there will be complaints such as housemaid's knee and aching backs to add to the problems of kennel ownership. Never overlook the usefulness of the watering can, either.

Garden hoses and convenient taps from which to run them, yes; unless you have already been involved in kennel work, however, you might not think of such items as pressure washers. These are industrial cleaning machines which can be used at low or high pressures, with hot or cold water or saturated steam; they may be used with a detergent, and can clean roofs and walls as well as floors. Naturally, inexperienced staff should not be expected to handle sophisticated equipment without training: steam cleaning may remove the paint and plaster as well as the dirt and germs!

Another cleaning item, essential in the kennel context, is the automatic washing machine. Small kennels may rely on the owner's washing machine to cope with the kennel laundry but the second-hand sales rooms may have some useful bargains in this type of equipment and it can be quite inexpensive. There will be bedding and towels to wash.

Disinfection

Disinfection should not be confused with sterilisation, which means the destruction of all living matter, or with disinfestation which is the destruction of vermin and pests. However, before disinfectants are brought into action on the kennel front, basic but thorough cleaning must be carried out. Dust, dirt, urine, faeces, coat and skin detritus are contaminants which may render some disinfectants inactive, as does the presence of detergent in certain cases. Antiseptics are products for use on the skin or living tissue and are not to be confused with products designed for cleaning floors, walls or utensils.

However major or minor the basic cleaning chores, surfaces should be rinsed clean of detergent and dried before the disinfecting process can be carried out efficiently. Too many kennel workers forget, or have never been taught, that cleaning comes before disinfecting, as dust and organic matter may render the disinfectant properties inactive.

Quarantine kennels, except in unusual cases, are not for beginners but may be in their plans for the future; they are required to use a disinfectant approved for use under the Diseases of Animals (Approved Disinfectants) Order 1978 (amended 1991).

As suggested in Chapter 5 (Laws and Orders) every boarding kennel owner should have a copy of the list of disinfectants approved by the Ministry of Agriculture, Fisheries and Food because the products listed therein have been officially tested. Several are available through distributors of products for use in kennels, whose advertisements will be found in the canine press. Also, the approved list gives the name of each disinfectant and the name and address of the proprietor. It is therefore a simple matter to contact them for information and advice on the use of particular products.

Products intended for agricultural use are not necessarily correct for use in small animal boarding establishments, but in some cases the same manufacturers also produce disinfectants specifically designed for use with dogs and cats. They have specific information regarding their use in domestic boarding kennels and catteries, and will advise you as to the chemical content of the disinfectant and of its correct dilution for its use in particular circumstances.

In all cases it should be remembered that disinfectants are dangerous substances and that kennel staff must be properly instructed in their use. Disinfectants require time to work, and such times should be given in the instructions for use and carefully followed. Fumes from disinfectants are hazardous and may cause respiratory problems in humans or animals. Liquids may soak into any impervious materials – that is unsealed wood, brick or concrete – and heat, either natural or applied, may cause fumes to be released. This is one reason why impervious materials are advised in kennel construction.

The Feline Advisory Bureau also publishes a comprehensive list of disinfectants and advises on their use in catteries. Some disinfectants which are suitable for use in canine accommodation are not suitable for use with cats. The boarding kennel and cattery owner's objective is optimum health within the establishment, and some individual research into this subject should be rewarding.

Chemical disinfectants

Disinfectant agents are either physical or chemical. Steam is a physical agent and may be used in the kennel environment in pressure cleaners. Chemical agents are contained in disinfectants found on supermarket shelves or supplied by firms specialising in kennel disinfectants. The labelling of domestic disinfectants is not universally good despite improvements in recent years. It is now a requirement to show the chemical contents on labels of disinfectant containers, warnings regarding their misuse and what remedial actions should be taken in such circumstances, but no domestic disinfectants actually suggest kennel use though some are suitable. Others may be safe with dogs but should not be used with cats. With one exception – bleach – it would be wiser to choose a disinfectant product specifically designed for use in kennels.

Each constituent of chemical disinfectants has its own characteristic; knowing how they should be used may help the boarding kennel owner to decide which products to choose. The efficiency of any disinfectant depends on several factors including, of course, the micro-organisms which it will be required to elimi-

nate, where the disinfectant is to be used and on what type of surface, whether it is toxic (poisonous) to some species, whether it
may cause corrosion, or damage or irritation to the skin and tissue,
and whether there is anything present in the environment (dirt,
detergent etc) which might inhibit its action. Two other factors
need to be considered – expense and the competence of the
person(s) who will be using the disinfectants. It should be stressed
to kennel staff that disinfectants are to be used strictly in accor-
dance with instructions, that dilutions must be correct, that one
disinfectant should never be mixed with another, and that dishwashing detergent should never be added to a disinfectant solution in the false hope that it will aid cleaning power. It will, in
most cases, simply render the disinfectant properties inactive!
Disinfectants generally work better in higher temperatures; therefore they should be added to hot water.

Disinfectant chemicals are classified into simple generic
groups: alkalis, alcohols, aldehydes, halogens, phenolics and surface-active agents. The groups from which the common disinfectants draw their constituents are the aldehydes (as formaldehyde
solution – formalin), the halogens (sodium hypochlorite solution
– bleach), and phenolics (phenol and its modern derivatives as
found in such products as Jeyes Fluid, Jeypine, Lysol, Dettol etc).
The surface-active agents may be subdivided into two groups:
quaternary ammonium compounds (Quats) and amphoteric/poly-
mer surface-active agents. The latter sub-group contains the most
modern of the disinfectant preparations which, being both disinfectant and detergent, excel at cleaning while simultaneously
annihilating the micro-organisms. Being non-toxic, non-corro-
sive, odourless, deodorising, harmless to the skin and not inactivated by organic matter, amphoteric/polymer surface-active
agents meet many of the needs of the boarding kennel/cattery
owner, and indeed are recommended for use in cat units. An
example of the preparations available in this group is Tego, which
is recommended by the Feline Advisory Bureau.

The more sophisticated disinfectants are combinations of various ingredients and are more expensive, but a properly protected
kennel saves money in the end. As micro-organisms tend to
develop resistance to chemicals, disinfectant formulae are always
being researched and updated and new products introduced.

Bleach

Sodium hypochlorite (bleach) is very effective and is in regular use as a disinfectant in the domestic environment. Domestos is a well-known example and the proprietors, Lever Brothers Ltd. may be contacted at Lever House, 3 St James Road, Kingston-upon-Thames, Surrey KT1 2BA. The Domestos information pack includes a leaflet on pet hygiene listing the following dilutions which may be of use in boarding establishments: 4 fluid ounces Domestos per gallon of water for soiling on outside paths, tiled or vinyl-covered floors and litter trays. Feeding bowls should be washed in hot, soapy water and then disinfected by soaking in a solution of 1 fluid ounce Domestos per gallon of water for about 10 minutes, then rinsed thoroughly and dried. The second dilution may also be used for disinfecting pet beds, bedding, grooming implements, and toys and bedding where appropriate. (*NB*. 1 fluid ounce = 25ml, 1 gallon = 4.5 litres.)

Please note that the above-mentioned dilutions refer only to Domestos, as not all bleaches have the same available sodium hypochlorite content. Another advantage is that to safeguard the environment Domestos breaks down rapidly after use into common salt, oxygen and other harmless substances. This underlines another point, namely that bleach should be mixed and used immediately, not left standing around for future use as it will become ineffective through oxidation, not to mention being a hazard to pets looking for a drink! Bleach must never be mixed with any other cleaner or dishwashing detergent and is inactivated by contact with organic matter, so if used in kennels and runs or litter trays, for example, these must be thoroughly cleaned of faeces, urine or other organic detritus before the bleach solution is used.

An ineffective use of bleach occurs when conscientious kennel owners, anxious to prevent visitors bringing infection into the kennels on their shoes, leave a doormat soaked in bleach at the kennel entrance. One pair of dirty shoes or boots on the bleach-soaked doormat inactivates the disinfectant properties, if indeed they have not already been inactivated by oxidation!

Bleach is readily available and comparatively inexpensive. It has many useful properties and some disadvantages, one being that it is not recommended for use on metal surfaces. However, there are advantages and disadvantages to all products which demonstrates why, to assist you in making an informed choice, it is necessary to know the constituents of disinfectants and how they work.

Phenol

The other generic group from which the constituents of many well-known and easily obtained disinfectants are drawn is the phenolic group. Phenol, popularly called carbolic acid, is a caustic poison and extremely toxic to living tissue. Some of the modern derivatives of phenol are xylenol, chloroxyphenol, orthophenylphenol and hexachlorophene; residues of these substances can be absorbed through the skin and some of them have been banned from use in products designed for human babies. They are all dangerous to cats and should never be used in catteries. Many disinfectants in this group are used in boarding kennels for dogs and there have been many cases of sore paws and other problems which could be attributed to the use, overuse or incorrect use of unsuitable disinfectants. If there is any doubt that a product contains phenol, remember that water turns milky white when phenol is added to it.

Points to watch

Labels on all disinfectant preparations must list their chemical ingredients. Some products carry labels stating they are 'safe in use', or 'safe when used as directed', of 'safe for general household use'. None found on general sale is labelled as being 'guaranteed harmless to pets'. Even if such claims were made some pets may be allergic to certain substances, and what may be suitable for dogs may mean death to cats. No boarding kennel owner, or anyone caring for animals, should purchase domestic disinfectants from any source without checking that the active ingredients are stated on the container. Proof of content, and official proof of testing in the small animal environment – not hearsay or salesmen's patter – are required because kennel owners' responsibility is towards the boarders in their care and to the owners of those animals.

Disinfectants with strong pine odours will soak into wood surfaces which have not been sealed, and should infra-red heat be used in the area, it will draw irritant fumes from the wood which may affect the pets' eyes.

It is most important to realise that dogs and cats in boarding kennels are of necessity confined to comparatively small spaces, and that apart from walking on surfaces which have been disinfected with possibly irritant chemicals, they may also lie on these surfaces; they may also lick themselves and thus ingest any disinfectant residue which adheres to their coats. Disinfected floors should always be rinsed with clean water and allowed to dry before the animal is put back into its kennel, and in our damp climate floor drying can be a problem. Direct heating to aid drying may cause fumes from an unsuitable disinfectant product. The incorrect use of certain disinfectants which are generally unsuitable for kennels may also make kennel floors sticky; this is mainly due to the breakdown of the chemical constituents and their subsequent lack of efficacy.

Another problem is that if kennel staff do not understand the correct use of disinfectants, and why the manufacturers' recommended dilutions should be strictly adhered to, they may add disinfectants to a bucket of water making a stronger solution, which is not only unnecessary and wasteful but also a potential danger to a susceptible animal. A disinfectant noted for its efficacy in one field should not be automatically considered ideal for use in another. The general lack of comprehensive information on disinfectants and our common acceptance of these products without question is still a problem despite improved labelling requirements.

When boarding dogs and cats, use only disinfectant products proved suitable in the small animal boarding environment. Check that the dilution rate for use in a small animal environment is clearly indicated, that the active ingredient(s) are named and that a remedial procedure in case of accidents is shown. Instruct all kennel staff in the careful use of disinfectants, as the object must be to reduce the risk of disease without introducing health risks from the disinfectant agent.

Newcomers to the kennel business may not be familiar with the use of disinfectants in spray form. The specialists in kennel and cattery disinfectants can provide information on this type of product which, when sprayed into the air, helps to reduce airborne infection. Do not confuse these sprays with aerosols which contain propellants, and which some animals absolutely loathe. An advantage of the spray disinfectants is the ease of use: spraying walls, floors etc is time- and work-saving. Kennel work is physically hard, and effective labour-saving methods in any department are worth consideration. A great disadvantage of any spray disinfectant is that some pets and people who breathe in sprayed droplets may suffer respiratory problems. Pets should not be present when spraying takes place, and kennel staff should wear masks.

Destroying worm eggs

There is one further useful, and some would say essential, item which a boarding kennel owner anxious to keep his establishment thoroughly disinfected should possess. This is the flame gun used for destroying weeds in the garden and it employs heat to destroy worm eggs. Much publicity has been given to the subject of *Toxocara canis* infection in children, and this is dealt with in more detail on page 70. It might be hoped that all conscientious pet owners worm their dogs regularly, but the hope that more efficient worm medicines for pets will be available in the future is much more likely to be realised.

The dogs in the boarding kennel may be shedding worm eggs, unknown to the kennel owners; the eggs are extremely tenacious of life, and can live even in raw concrete which is porous! Using a concrete sealant simply means that instead of invading the concrete, the worm eggs will be flushed off the sealed surface by the cleaning water or disinfectant and take up residence elsewhere. Disinfectants, unfortunately, do not kill sticky worm eggs, which can, however, be annihilated with a flame gun. Unsealed concrete runs can be treated annually with a flame gun after the main boarding season and when no dogs are around; this will remove the worm egg danger completely. When concrete runs or other stone surfaces have been sealed, it is necessary to check where the water runs off. Does it go straight down a drain? Does it run into a gravel soakaway which can be flame gunned? Never embark on this annual operation unless all conditions are right and the hose is connected and ready, in case of fire.

Insecticides

Insecticidal products are frequently used in conjunction with cleaning and disinfection, though not necessarily so. How much your kennel property is affected by flies, wasps and other airborne insects may depend on your daily cleaning routine, or by proximity to a farm, or neighbour, whose attention to cleanliness is not as good as yours, or to other factors altogether. Again, it should be borne in mind that boarders are in a confined space, so spray the animal accommodation while the pets are outside! Insecticidal sprays need to be used with caution and the best choices are from the products made by the specialist kennel disinfection firms. Be sure that you and your staff know the difference between the various kennel air sprays, and when and how to use them. Never use any spray when there is food around, and always resist picking up the handy aerosol for a quick burst against flying intruders without considering what else is going on in the kennel. Many people, suspicious of the presence of too many chemicals sprayed into the atmosphere, prefer to use the old-fashioned sticky fly papers. These simple, unsightly but harmless objects are not easy to find these days, though they are usually advertised in the summer months in the weekly dog papers; kennel folk must be good customers.

Exterior cleaning

Having dealt with the interior cleaning of kennels, the same routine procedures can be applied to the runs attached to them. Ideally, each kennel should have its own adjoining run with free access. Even so, that is not sufficient for thorough exercise and the dogs look forward to a gallop in the larger paddock, where they are taken individually.

The large runs may be grassed, and if they are big enough they do not get too badly churned up in wet weather. Many dogs will not urinate or defaecate except on grass; the disadvantage is the cleaning up! Some large exercise areas are surfaced with gravel or, better still, with washed pea beach. To surface large areas with concrete is costly and although they are the easiest to clean satisfactorily, dogs are usually much happier playing on grass, with gravel – once they learn to trust its surface – coming second.

Though grass or gravel runs may please the dogs best, there is no way at all that they can be perfectly disinfected however diligent the owner and kennel staff. Obviously, faeces should be removed from outside runs as frequently as necessary, and provided these are solid the task is not too difficult. The problems arise if a dog is afflicted with diarrhoea which may be caused simply by stress while settling into new surroundings or, more seriously, by an illness. As it is impossible to tell immediately whether illness is the cause of the looseness, it is better to restrict the dog to an isolation kennel and clean and disinfect as required. This further points up the argument for having kennels with runs attached. Grass runs can be sprinkled with disinfectant applied from a watering can but efficient disinfection is an impossibility.

The same applies to gravel, but regular 'picking up' as the expression is, plus spraying with the hose, will keep problems to a minimum.

Sterilisation of feeding and drinking bowls

A further daily cleaning routine is the proper cleansing and sterilisation of feeding and drinking bowls. A sterilising detergent is most useful here and is a time saver; it ensures a quick and thorough job. Otherwise, bowls can be washed in ordinary detergent, rinsed in clean water, then rinsed in a sodium hypochlorite solution and rinsed again before feeding time. Ideally each dog should have its own food and water bowls as a further precaution against passing on infections; alternatively, disposable dishes are available and these are particularly useful for cats.

The automatic dishwasher for kennel use has probably not yet been invented, but a commercial or domestic dishwasher is by far the most hygienic way of washing dishes and it is possible to pick up second-hand ones cheaply.

Disposal problems

The kennel owner's first disposal problem is how to cope with the inevitable daily accumulation of excrement, which is an inescapable fact of kennel life. Other kennel routines have some bearing on this problem, as does the question of whether or not your kennel is on main drainage or has its own cesspool or septic tank drainage. Kennel waste disposal is without doubt a major subject which new kennel owners need to study.

The first consideration should be how certain kennel routines may assist, or complicate, disposal problems. The choice of bedding material has a bearing on this subject, as has the use of newspapers or other coverings on kennel floors. The boarders which are pet dogs, one might fairly presume to have been house-trained; those which are strictly kennel dogs, from breeding kennels for example, may not be house-trained though they should certainly be kennel clean; much depends on how their owners have educated them. There may be times when your boarding kennel cares for show dogs or breeding stock, as breeders/exhibitors need holiday breaks too and assistance in times of illness. The kennel owner who is connected with the dog show world will know what to expect behaviourwise from kennel dogs as opposed to household pets; the newcomer without this experience will have to learn the hard way.

The best trained household pet, when subjected to stress, such as being marched off to the kennel, may suffer tummy upsets, and then suffer further stress because it has made a mess in its kennel. Rebukes for such mistakes are not to be administered in the boarding environment, where understanding of the reasons and a building of confidence as the boarder settles down improve the situation. Kennel owners and workers have to accept the fact that these least pleasant chores are most important. Working with animals involves all their care in sickness and in health: looking after the animals' living quarters, and the rewarding, unpleasant and, at times, foul jobs which are part of total care.

Beds and bedding

Pets in the boarding environment need to be happy, and bringing their own bedding keeps them in touch with home comforts. Some owners may even bring their pet's bed too, but you should always have available bedding and beds of varying sizes. It is also helpful when owners bring their pet's towel, but the wise kennel owner keeps a stock of towels on hand anyway – a spell of wet weather means a lot of wet dogs. Short-haired breeds are quickly dried but some of the long-haired varieties need careful drying and, in fact, the use of an electric dog dryer simplifies this task and is a worthwhile purchase. Floor-standing electric dog dryers are, of course, standard equipment in the grooming parlour.

Bedding needs to be kept clean, and is not shared with other boarders unless two dogs from the same family are kennelled together. Sending a boarder home with soiled bedding will not endear you to the owner, which is bad for business, so your washing machine will be kept busy. A tumble dryer is virtually a necessity. Blankets are useful, and polyester 'fur' bedding is particularly cosy and comfortable and is fully washable. Flame-retardant materials exist and are an added bones, as fire risks must be kept to a minimum. Because of the risk of fire, certain types of bedding should not be used in small animal boarding establishments. These include wood wool, shredded paper and straw, which may also harbour insects. Kennel bedding suppliers are noted in the Appendix.

Boarding kennel owners, and the boarders' owners too, need to be warned that some dogs in kennels are particularly destructive and set to work on reducing their bedding to shreds and wreck their beds if possible. Pet owners seldom take such things into account when they complain about your boarding fees! Some modern kennel designs include fibreglass beds which fold up into the walls giving more kennel floor space – but if your kennel is so equipped bear in mind that a dog needs something to rest on during the day.

Fibreglass is a 'warm' material and is also used for conventional beds which then need little if any bedding. Oval plastic beds are available in all sizes, stack well when not in use and are easy to scrub, but can get chewed around the edges. Remember that frayed edges of plastic beds will harbour germs just as do chewed edges of plastic feeding dishes. What is not so obvious is that beds with frayed edges will collect hair, particularly from long-coated breeds. There is something to be said for encouraging clients to bring their pets' own beds!

Floor coverings

Strictly speaking, the impervious and properly cleaned and dry kennel floor should need no additional covering. Whatever you put down as a floor covering will rapidly become untidy, if not ripped to pieces. However, there are occasions when some sort of covering may be needed and most kennels keep a stock of newspapers for such purposes. These can be saved from your household, scrounged from neighbours and friends, brought in by clients or begged from your bank which takes *The Times* and the *Financial Times* (very absorbent!) Newsprint is mildly biocidal, which is an advantage, but unfortunately printer's ink will discolour light-coloured coats and make white dogs positively grubby.

Other points against the use of newspaper are the fire risk and the disposal problem. However, it is particularly useful for puppies whose ideas of toilet training may revert to the newspaper stage, and in cases of illness. Your isolation unit should have a supply in readiness. Needless to say, used newspaper should be destroyed, preferably by incineration.

Resist the temptation to scatter sawdust or wood chips on kennel floors even though you may have seen such things in kennels which you have visited. The fire hazard rules these materials out, and there is an added risk of sawdust getting into dogs' coats or eyes and setting up skin irritations. If sawdust is used at all it should only be from softwoods which have not been treated with wood preservatives. Products used for treating timber can be toxic to animals, and this should also be borne in mind if wooden cattery buildings are used. If possible avoid the use of bedding materials and floor coverings which are potentially dangerous, create a disposal problem and therefore cause you extra work.

Incineration

Incineration used to be an acceptable method for the disposal of kennel waste, but recently much more emphasis has been accorded to air pollution and this method of disposal may not now be approved in some areas. Therefore, whether you are starting your own boarding kennel or are purchasing an existing business, the subject of the disposal of kennel waste is an extremely important matter for consideration. In the case of an existing business, check whether the disposal methods used by the seller are approved by the local environmental health department, and if not find out what system would meet official approval. If you are starting your own kennel, discuss the waste disposal system with your environmental health officer before becoming involved. If possible, check with other boarding kennels regarding the efficacy of approved disposal systems. Do not underestimate the waste disposal volume from a busy boarding kennel and/or cattery, and remember that kennel and cattery waste awaiting disposal must also be contained so that it does not attract flies. Heavy duty black plastic bags may serve as temporary containers, but keep them out of sight if possible. Regular disposal of kennel waste is vitally important.

Cesspool and septic tank

One other competent disposal method for kennel excrement is via the septic tank or cesspool, not by the main drainage system. Main drainage services are for domestic waste and surface water only.

The cesspool which serves either the house or the kennels will need to be emptied by the local council or a private sewage disposal contractor, for which a charge will be made. The septic tank is a tank in which the solid matter of continuously flowing sewage is disintegrated by bacteria. These tanks have an overflow of clear water, usually draining down to a stream or ditch. In theory a septic tank is not supposed to need emptying, but in fact most require periodic emptying. If the property you have taken over has septic tank drainage for kennel use, check the capacity of the tank – or rather, ask the chap who comes to empty it unless the capacity is listed elsewhere. Modern detergents, disinfectants and other chemicals play a part in inhibiting the bacterial action, which should keep the septic tank trouble free. The new country dweller needs to study rural drainage. Knowing how to cope with previously unfamiliar systems will help to obviate problems. Check where the pipes run; note where the overflow and soak-away are located; such areas can become overgrown with grass or nettles. In fact, a particularly luscious grass or weed growth in an otherwise sparse area should alert the warning signals in your brain. Check that an overflow is not blocked: if it is, seek help without delay.

It stands to reason that if they are available and working properly, septic tanks are the most convenient and least unpleasant means of kennel excrement disposal. However, no drains can be used for the disposal of soiled newspaper, sawdust, wood chips or cat litter, which must be burned. Companies specialising in kennel design and equipment have up-to-date information on modern disposal systems.

Refuse collection or burial

Dustbins and garbage sacks are other items of necessity. Not everything can be burned or disposed of via the septic tank. If canned dog or cat food is used, and some surely will be, the empty tins are for the refuse collectors. These tins can amount to a size-able problem; one way of reducing the tin mountain is by opening the tin at both ends and then crushing it flat, which saves a great deal of space. Naturally, any refuse which has to await council collection should be in containers with tight lids. The local population of wild creatures, including foxes and badgers, will otherwise raid the garbage.

One further method of disposing of kennel waste is by burial. This is the most laborious and time-consuming operation and is often dependent on the right digging conditions or how much ground there is available. It can be satisfactory but is better avoided unless some member of the kennel crew wants to spend all his days digging. Other methods of disposal exist, none acceptable, and in fact, some kennel owners prefer to remain secretive about their methods which may therefore be viewed with suspicion. Never continue a highly suspect method of disposal just because your predecessor got away with it. Remember this is a health subject.

Human considerations

Though the boarders come first, the humans owning or employed at the kennel deserve consideration too. The work is physically hard, which many enjoy; it is also repetitive, which some may find boring at times. The fact that the physical chores of cleaning and caring involve bending, stretching, lifting, carrying and being on the go all day means that muscles may be over-used and complain. Learn to pace yourself and, though diligent and conscientious, do not become a workaholic. Everyone deserves a break and works better afterwards. The temptation, when working for oneself, is to drive on and on, perhaps not realising what is happening until that nasty feeling of exhaustion has to be heeded. Remembering the creative side to any job – that is, making the business work and prosper while seeing your boarders well and happy – offsets some tensions which, unalleviated, cause tiredness. Job satisfaction is important but so is recreation.

Clothing

Clothing should provide comfort and protection, and appearance needs to be thought of too. Clothes chosen for their usefulness need not look as if they are the dregs of a jumble sale. Jeans and track suits can be neat and tidy, as can shirts and sweaters. Wellington boots are a necessity, and comfortable rainwear gets a lot of use in our damp climate. Changes of clothing are necessary in really bad weather, and if you have live-in kennel staff, means of washing and drying clothing in a hurry is vitally important. Tee shirts and tabard overalls can be very colourful and attractive. Simple styles in easy care fabrics are essential.

Pollutants

Although kennel owners and staff are not confined to the relatively small quarters assigned to the pets, they are exposed to cleaning and disinfecting materials, insect sprays and air fresheners every working day. The boarders stay for only a limited time; the staff carry on regardless. Some people, and some dogs, are allergic to these substances.

When cleaning kennels, or in fact in any cleaning demanding the use of disinfectants, it is unwise to put bare hands into the disinfectant mixture. Provide rubber gloves and rubber boots. Consider carefully your choice of chemical cleaners – again your most comprehensive advice will come from firms specialising in the manufacture of products for kennel use. Where possible choose sprays which are not aerosols: the use of aerosols should be limited if they cannot be avoided completely. If flea aerosols have to be used, try to do this in the open air and not in the confined space of a kennel, and warn kennel assistants to avoid breathing the spray. A pet owner spraying one dog occasionally is far less exposed to pollutant chemicals than the kennel worker involved with a number of dogs needing flea treatment. Insufficient publicity has been given so far to the health of workers in this trade.

Safety first

Keeping up appearances is important, so painting and decorating will form a large part of the kennel maintenance work, though not in the busiest boarding weeks. Many of the modern redecorating products are hazardous from the point of view of fumes, and every effort should be made to obtain non-toxic products when possible. No lead-based paints, please, and to save work remember that, as kennel painting is an oft-repeated task, a good covering of one coat of emulsion will do just as well as a fancier product needing two coats or more.

All decorating and maintenance supplies and tools need to be kept in a place of safety, as do all bulk supplies of disinfectants. These are simply sensible precautions so that you know where to find what you want when you need it – which will usually be immediately – and to prevent accidental misuse of any products which might be harmful to humans and dogs.

Fire

Fire precautions should be observed at all times, and fire extinguishers sited according to the recommendations of your local fire prevention officer whose advice can be obtained by a telephone call to the Fire Department.

Every kennel should bear a large NO SMOKING sign, and this should be rigidly enforced and observed by owners, staff and visitors. Not only is there a fire risk but cigarette smoke is yet one more air pollutant which should not be inflicted on pets or people. This is one hazard which you can eliminate totally from your kennel.

Tetanus

All people connected with kennel work should make sure that their tetanus inoculations are in order. Consult your own doctor about this, and make sure that all your staff are protected too. Tetanus immunisation is necessary as cuts and scratches are sure to beset kennel workers from a variety of causes, and animal bites are not the least of these. Dogs and cats should be handled properly to prevent bites and scratches, and it must always be remembered that a frightened animal may react quickly and in a way unlike its normal behaviour. Teeth and claws carry germs, and in the event of a kennel worker being bitten or scratched, prompt washing of even the smallest wound with soap or detergent is essential and may prevent infection setting in. Cat bites and scratches often cause more severe reactions than expected, so wise precautions are an obvious necessity.

First aid boxes

Although the owner takes all precautions against major accidents, there are sure to be minor ones. As well as a boarders' first aid box (ask your vet to advise on the contents of this) there should be a staff first aid box too. Equip the latter with some antiseptic solution, sterile dressings, an eye bath, band-aids, scissors and whatever you consider necessary for first aid treatment. Include a note showing the local doctor's telephone number, as it will save time looking it up in the directory if you have to make an appointment in a hurry. Most injuries are minor, but in the case of bites a doctor's advice should be sought.

Alternative medical care

Working in kennels is demanding and repetitive and may lead to strains and sprains or 'slipped discs'. To assist a fast return to work, effective treatment for such injuries may be given by a chiropractor or osteopath, and it is not usually necessary to be referred to a practitioner by your doctor. Consult the Yellow Pages. Fully qualified chiropractors have the letters DC after their names and are members of the British Chiropractic Association. Fully qualified osteopaths bear the letters DO MRO which signify membership of the General Council and Register of Osteopaths. Newer members of these professions may also have a Bachelor of Science degree. Though not available under the NHS, such treatments are not excessively expensive and emergencies are usually seen without delay. Getting back to work quickly can save you money.

Zoonoses and other ailments

Zoonoses are diseases which are transmissible from animals to man. The most widely publicised of these is rabies and our quarantine kennels are our front line defence against this dreadful disease. Every kennel owner should obtain the Feline Advisory Bureau's paper entitled Zoonoses, a copy of which should be in every kennel and cattery in the country. Do not be misled into thinking that this publication is only for cat enthusiasts. Some zoonoses have received an overdose of publicity considering their relatively low incidence. A few of them are mentioned here, but for detailed information please obtain the FAB paper.

Ringworm

Both dogs and cats may be infected with ringworm, a skin disease, and this is readily transmitted to man from the animals, but not from man to man. To be awkward, ringworm spores may not cause the dog or cat to show any symptoms, though infected animals can be diagnosed by the veterinary surgeon using an ultraviolet light known as a Wood's lamp. Any such infections, should they be attributed to your kennel, must be dealt with under veterinary direction, as it is a sure business loser apart from being an undesirable health risk and unpleasant for the sufferers.

Nematode worms

Everybody knows that dogs and cats have worms and that in comparatively rare cases – and they are quite rare despite occasional alarmist publicity in the national press – a child may be affected by toxocariasis. The nematode worms, *Toxocara canis* and *Toxocara cati*, occur in dogs and cats and are passed in their faeces. Unfortunately, these eggs can survive in a viable state for several years. Adult animals may get worms by ingesting infective eggs, or by eating small mammals which are infected, and puppies and kittens become infected before they are born or as suckling babies. If man accidentally ingests the eggs there may be infection of the central nervous system, or a sense organ such as the eye, resulting in partial or complete blindness. Some cases are reported annually in the UK and children are particularly vulnerable if they play in gardens or areas fouled by dogs. Uncontrolled dogs foul children's play areas in parks and this has resulted in the banning of dogs from some parks and beaches. It is unlikely that children would become infected at your kennels as they will not be playing in the dog runs, and your hygiene programme should minimise risks to visitors. Kennel owners are experts in cleaning up; most pet owners ignore the necessity!

Fleas

Dogs and cats have fleas. All dogs and cats may catch fleas from hedgehogs, or from each other, and fleas also bite people. It seems that human females are more likely to be the target of flea bites than human males. Some people react quite strongly to flea bites, others seem to be less bothered. Some dogs are extremely sensitive to flea allergens and suffer skin eruptions of the wet eczema type. Fleas are adaptable creatures and many a comfortable, centrally heated home has become a flea haven as fleas do not spend all their time aboard the animal but return for a quick meal as required. Wage war on fleas, as neither humans nor animals enjoy their company. Fleas live in carpets and in cracks between floor boards or in nooks and crannies in kennels.

Cheyletiella mange mite

Another minute pest has caused many people connected with small animal care a great deal of trouble because the real problem has often been difficult to diagnose. This is the cheyletiella mange mite which may be suspected if a dog is very scurfy around the head and neck, is itchy and if, after cuddling such an animal, the human develops a rash similar to a crop of mosquito bites. Not everyone is allergic to the bites of the cheyletiella mite, though many owners who cuddle an infested puppy will be bitten on the arms and trunk, and on the thighs if they have let the puppy sit on their lap. These mites can be abolished by using a prescribed preparation such as Quellada veterinary shampoo; the cheyletiella mite also infests rabbits: hence its other name, the rabbit fur mite, and the difficulty of eliminating it.

Toxoplasmosis

Toxoplasmosis is another disease which has received wide publicity recently and although infections with *Toxoplasma gondii*, a protozoan parasite, are common in man, the actual clinical disease is rare. Cats can play a key role in this disease as they may acquire infective cysts from meat and later shed infective oocysts in their faeces. The cat may show no symptoms whatsoever. Man may also acquire infection by eating cystic forms in meat, particularly if it is insufficiently cooked, and serological surveys indicate that

30 to 60 per cent of the adult human population have encountered the infection. However, it is important for pregnant women to avoid infection and they are made aware of this in literature pertaining to their condition. They should avoid handling cat litter.

Sarcoptic mange

Sarcoptic mange occurs in dogs and is transmissible to man in the form of scabies. This type of mange usually starts on the dog's muzzle and spreads backwards. When any skin conditions are noted in the dog or cat boarders, veterinary advice should be sought and the owner informed. It is surprising how many people think their pets are simply enjoying a good scratch without ever checking to see why they are scratching or uncomfortable.

Salmonella

The salmonella groups of bacteria are usually the culprits in most cases of food poisoning in man; such bacteria may be excreted by carrier animals who are quite well themselves, and most pets could be a possible source of infection. Fresh meat is also a possible source of salmonella and should always be handled with care, all cutting and preparation utensils being sterilised. There should never be direct contact between pet meat and meat intended for human consumption, or between cooked and raw meat.

It is, of course, important to be aware of the diseases which can be transmitted from animals to mankind but it is also important not to become obsessed by them. Proper, hygienic handling and attention to cleanliness can eliminate most dangers, and taking action against parasites can destroy that particular problem. The most difficult cases are those in which a person is allergic to cats or dogs in general and may suffer from asthma as a result. This cannot be called a true zoonosis, but it is a fact which cannot be ignored. Some people who are allergic to cats or dogs may have a reaction similar to hay fever but, as with asthma allergy, tests by a doctor can determine the cause of the reactions. Unfortunately, such people cannot work with cats and dogs.

Immunisation

There is one rule concerning your kennel which must never be broken – not even slightly bent; no boarders should ever be accepted without positive proof of vaccination. Not only should the boarders be vaccinated against the prevalent infectious diseases but the immunisation record should show that it was carried out within the previous 12 months. When a dog or cat is vaccinated by a veterinary surgeon a certificate of vaccination is given to the owner; this will indicate the date of the vaccination, the vaccine which was used and its batch number, and the diseases against which the pet was vaccinated. Accept no excuses for nonpresentation of this document.

Dogs should have a certificate indicating that they have been immunised against canine parvovirus disease, distemper, hardpad and leptospirosis. Cats' certificates should indicate immunisation against feline enteritis and feline influenza. Should a vaccination certificate be within a short time of its renewal date when the pet's holiday booking is made, it would be sensible to advise the owner to consult the veterinary surgeon about the booster dose being given before the animal arrives at your kennel. A new location is always a challenge germ-wise, and boarding is also stressful for the pet when it may be more vulnerable to disease than it would be in its own home surroundings.

In recent years parvovirus disease in dogs has been a major problem and when it first struck there was no specific vaccine for canines. However, great advances have now been made and boarding kennel owners should keep abreast of new developments in the prevention and treatment of infectious diseases. Regular news of this type is published in the weekly trade papers.

At the time of writing, the consensus is that puppies which have been inoculated against canine parvovirus disease at 8 and 12 weeks should be inoculated again at 18 or 20 weeks of age as it appears that some puppies carry a maternal immunity longer than others; if this inherent immunity is still present when a vaccination is given it renders the vaccine ineffective. When in doubt seek a veterinary surgeon's advice. In the world of dogs it is generally the exhibition fraternity who are more aware of this, as their dogs are exposed to greater disease risks at shows. It is also possible that the pet dog which is taken for 'walkies' at the earliest possible opportunity may have acquired a certain 'street' immunity not shared by the more protected show pup. However, should you be asked to board a puppy, and dogs are puppies until they are a year old, check the date of its parvovirus vaccination and if there is any question in your mind about adequate protection, ask the vet about a booster injection.

There are many canine and feline illnesses of which boarding kennel owners should be aware but it is not their job to diagnose or prescribe treatment for any ailments. This is the province of the veterinary surgeon and it is illegal for an unqualified person to infringe. However, should the owner of a pet which boards with you provide medication prescribed by the dog's or cat's vet it is your duty to make certain the vet's instructions are carried out. If a boarding kennel owner is not familiar with such conditions in dogs as pancreatitis, which involves a special diet, or diabetes, which may involve daily injections, it would be better to refuse such clients until sufficient knowledge and expertise in dealing with these cases have been acquired.

The most important observations a boarding kennel owner must be competent to make concerning a dog's or cat's health on arrival are whether there are obvious signs of illness. Does the animal look well? Does it have poorly eyes, a runny nose? Is it coughing? Limping? Has it any sores? Is it scratching itself? It is also important to realise that a dog which appears to be perfectly well on arrival may be incubating a disease which will manifest itself during the time it is boarding with you. The same warning applies to cats, but there is nothing you can do about this except to be aware that it might happen and, should it happen, take immediate action: isolate the pet and call the vet! Then follow his instructions to the letter.

Kennel cough

The bane of a kennel owner's life is kennel cough – a term which describes an upper respiratory infection only too commonly found in kennels. The chief symptom is, as the name suggests, a cough which may be aggravated by exercise or excitement, or possibly by apprehension. Sometimes it is a harsh dry cough, occasionally more like a choking cough but unfortunately, it is often a long-lasting cough and the boarder which goes home coughing and spluttering will not endear your establishment to his owner. Discuss with your vet what you can do to minimise the risks of kennel cough, and remember that this disease is hardest on very young or elderly dogs. Kennel cough is highly infectious and veterinary advice should be sought immediately, both for the sake of treating the sufferers and to prevent the disease spreading if possible. Do not be tempted to ignore it, and discuss with your vet the possibility of vaccination against this disease.

The major cause of kennel cough, tracheobronchitis, is *Bordetella bronchiseptica* and dogs can be protected by an intranasal vaccine, Intrac, which protects for up to six months. Unfortunately, recovered dogs remain infectious for several months; therefore it is wise for all boarders to be protected.

Stress

Probably the most common cause of illness among the residents in a boarding kennel is stress. The pet is, without its consent, removed from its familiar surroundings and people, taken from its usual animal, human and geographical contacts and deposited in a different environment in close association with strange animals. Its mental and physical reactions are challenged. Stress reactions may vary in small animals as they do in the human animal: the animal is disturbed, it may be resentful, frightened and feel really ill. Hopefully it will settle down, perhaps with a little extra attention at first, and then thoroughly enjoy its holiday.

What sort of stress reactions might you expect from a dog or cat? Apart from an obvious wariness of the new surroundings there may be an initial refusal of food. If the refusal continues, then special care has to be initiated. Perhaps the dog or cat does not like the food offered, and it is for this reason that your booking form should include the question regarding the animal's usual diet. Sometimes an extra tasty titbit may induce the boarder to start its meal. Occasionally very special attention may be needed, in which case hand feeding is sometimes necessary for it not only ensures that some food is taken but it gives the stressed boarder that extra loving contact which it is obviously missing.

Stress can bring a bitch into season, though she may not be due; it can also have the opposite effect and a bitch arriving in season may promptly finish. Diarrhoea may be another stress symptom. No symptom should be lightly dismissed: if there is no rapid improvement veterinary advice should be sought.

Ear problems

A dog's ears should not be itchy, sore, smelly or discharging. If they are, seek advice. Do not start pouring powders or squirting gooey liquids into a dog's ears unless you know why, otherwise you could make the problem worse. It is not your job to diagnose or prescribe treatment. Remember that.

Eczema

Dogs which come to board with you may not appear to be suffering from stress, or at least not as far as you can see. Unfortunately, they may suffer inwardly and sometimes skin eruptions occur. Also the presence of fleas may cause some dogs to break out in 'wet eczema', a nasty, oozing, painful sore patch. Such dogs may be reacting to flea allergens. Seek veterinary advice right away. Certain antibiotics work particularly well on the skin and your vet will know what to prescribe.

Eye problems

Eyes should be bright and alert. If they are runny, dull or the 'haw' (third eyelid or nictitating membrane) is showing, be suspicious. This is particularly important in cats, but in any case be watchful and ask the vet's advice.

Medication and dangerous substances

Never give medicines to any dog or cat without specific instructions either from the owner who leaves a prescription with you or from your own veterinary surgeon. Medicines affect different dogs in different ways – a pill which may leave a small Poodle still active may send a large Afghan to sleep immediately. What suits one breed may be a disaster for the next. Medicine suitable for dogs may spell death for cats. Even simple diarrhoea mixtures which soothe one patient may merely mask the symptoms of a serious complaint in others, or could even kill a cat.

Though you may notice worms in a dog's or cat's faeces you, as a boarding kennel owner, are not entitled to prescribe or administer medication without advice, and this is important, for worm medicines have been known to have adverse reactions. Do not take chances; take advice. Never look on a medicine as being harmless and beneficial to all species.

Apart from the irresponsible use of disinfectants, insect sprays etc and the dangers of drugs and medicines mentioned above, other dangerous substances which your boarders could come into contact with are herbicides (if you have used weedkillers), paints (if you have used lead-based paints), and creosote (which might have been used to preserve wooden buildings or fence posts).

Dangerous dogs

The Dangerous Dogs Bill enacted in 1991 placed restrictions on the importation, breeding and owning of Pit Bull Terriers which are bred as fighting dogs, and the Japanese Tosa, of which only one example was imported into England. There are provisions in the Bill to add other breeds should it be deemed necessary.

Whereas the Bill itself may not affect the boarding kennel owner who is not personally involved with any breed initially restricted, much publicity has been given to terrible cases of people, and young children in particular, being savaged by large, powerful breeds such as the Rottweiler, the German Shepherd Dog and other dogs of the guarding breeds. However, not all big dogs are dangerous. For example, the Guide Dogs for the Blind Association successfully uses large dogs, German Shepherds, Labradors, Golden Retrievers and crosses of the last two breeds when properly trained.

Unfortunately, human social problems have tempted some owners with little or no knowledge of training to acquire 'guard dogs' which are kept in a domestic environment unsuited to the dog's temperament. Any dog when challenged, startled, provoked or tempted is liable to bite, and aggressive large dogs with powerful jaws can inflict terrible damage. It is the few dogs which have reacted dangerously in certain circumstances, whether provoked or not, which inevitably have created a bad name for their breed in general. Small dogs are just as ready to use their sharp teeth in defence or aggression in certain circumstances.

How should the boarding kennel owner deal with dangerous dogs?

1. First, remember that not all members of so termed 'dangerous' breeds are aggressive, and second, never forget that any dog may bite.
2. Dogs tend to jump up when they bite, the larger the dog the more powerful its jaws and the higher it can spring.
3. A lone dog in a single-person household may become very possessive of its owner and may resent attention from others such as kennel assistants.
4. Two or three dogs which live happily together at home, and therefore may be kennelled together, may fight in your boarding kennel. Anyone who interferes between fighting dogs is almost certain to be bitten!
5. Dogs, particularly males, may act aggressively towards a male dog in a neighbouring run, and therefore to anyone who interferes. Move one of these dogs to another kennel.
6. The management of dogs, dangerous or not, is simplified in kennels which have attached runs with access via a hatch which can be controlled from outside the kennel. Kennel doors which have provision for placing food and water

bowls in position without the attendant having to enter the kennel itself are both time saving and a protection against aggression from the occupant. 'Guardsman' kennel gates are constructed on this principle.

Difficult pets

There are, unfortunately, some pets which are very difficult to handle. Though you may prefer to refuse to board certain breeds, some quite innocent looking pets may display bizarre or dangerous behaviour unexpectedly. For example, the author was once severely bitten by a tiny toy dog and the owner's only comment was, 'He's such a brave wee doggie; he sometimes sits on the stairs and won't let us go up or down.' Bad behaviour in their pets is often tolerated, or even encouraged, by unwise owners.

Normal pets are sociable creatures and, while an instinct to protect their property is understandable, unwarranted or unpredictable behaviour towards humans is unacceptable. Sometimes illness, a brain tumour for example, may cause behavioural changes in a dog. Some dogs may be disturbed by strange surroundings, your boarding kennel for example.

There are timid dogs and nervous dogs, and kennel staff should be trained to notice any change in a boarder's behaviour. Much more research has been done recently into the subject of animal behaviour and a book such as *Think Dog* by the late John Fisher, published by H F & G Witherby Ltd, and available from *Our Dogs*, gives valuable insight into dog behaviour and much advice regarding the handling of difficult dogs.

While most cats are placid pets a few may be very nervous and require gentle care. There are also a few cats which can be very resentful, or even downright spiteful, in strange surroundings. Again, this bad behaviour may be tolerated by their owners. A pair of heavy gauntlets is a useful protection from sharp claws!

Chapter 7

Feeding the Boarders

The boarding kennel owner should understand the nutritional needs of dogs and cats; remember that when they arrive at the kennels they will be under stress and that animals, like people, react to it in different ways.

Kennel owners whose booking application forms require details of the pet's usual food report that the majority of dogs and cats are fed on canned food, plus, in the case of dogs, a biscuit mixer meal or wholemeal bread – foods which are available at every local grocery store or supermarket, and not a bad feeding programme provided good quality brands are chosen. Naturally there will be some owners who feed their dogs on the best steak, offer nothing but liver or fillet of sole thinking, quite erroneously, that their pets are having the best. Others will use butchers' 'pet mince', a food of variable, and sometimes doubtful, value. Some pet owners, when preparing for their holiday, empty the family refrigerator of its collection of leftovers and feed them all to the dog in case it does not get a good meal in their absence! This means the pet may arrive on your doorstep full of unaccustomed goodies, and the initial shock of finding itself 'abandoned' by master or mistress may result in the pet starting its holiday with a very upset tummy. Owners may arrive with dog or cat and a carton of food, explaining that it is the only thing the pet will eat, or that it is the only food which does not give it diarrhoea. Surprisingly enough, the pet usually does very well on your kennel feed, but at least its home menu is there if required, and would of course be given if circumstances so dictated.

Another group of boarders falls into the special diet category. These may be dogs with pancreatic diseases or diabetes, or those on an obesity diet. Their diets will have been prescribed by veterinary surgeons and must be adhered to without deviation; these dogs may also require prescribed medication. You may impose special charges in such cases, or you may prefer not to cope with such problems. Sometimes it is preferable for a pet under treatment to be boarded with a veterinary surgeon as a hospital patient, but boarding kennel owners who have had experience in small animal care or animal nursing should be able to cope very well.

It sometimes happens that a client will claim that the pet will eat only an extravagant diet. In such situations, it is better to invite the pet owner to bring the food along; packed in daily portions and stored in a freezer it will present no bother to the kennel owner though again, some may consider making an extra charge for 'special services'. It is also quite likely that, given the opportunity, the pet may thoroughly enjoy what all the other boarders are lapping up at mealtimes. Nevertheless, allowances must be made for pet food fads, and in some cases the customer really is right.

Your basic kennel feed needs to be palatable, nutritious, economical and easy to prepare and serve. Most adult dogs in normal health are used to being fed once a day, though there may be a few exceptions, with perhaps a biscuit or two either first thing in the morning or last thing at night depending on the scheduled time of the main meal. Cats in normal health should be fed twice daily, but much more care is needed in planning their diets as they tend to suffer more from stress, particularly if they are boarded in a mixed kennel. Very young or elderly dog or cat boarders may need to be fed smaller quantities more frequently.

Some boarding kennels prefer to feed the dogs twice a day, early in the morning and in the late afternoon. They feel that this keeps the pets more contented and is also a precaution against bloat, or torsion, to which some breeds are particularly prone. Feeding only one main meal a day may lead to some dogs bolting their food, perhaps swallowing a lot of air in their hurry and thus causing discomfort or, at worst, bloat. Such a routine may mean that you should board fewer dogs, or employ more help. Either decision could necessitate a rise in your charges, but while there are pet owners who think all boarding fees are too high there are many others who appreciate the extra care and attention given to their pets and are willing to pay for it. Needless to say all dogs must be checked after each meal when you collect their empty dishes, and before bedtime, whatever feeding schedule you decide upon.

Types of pet food

Boarding kennel owners are now able to rely solely on manu-factured pet foods should they wish to do so, and the cooking of pet foods and its attendant odours can be eliminated from the kennel chores. Not that all kennels will wish to cut out the cooking;

it may depend on whether they have available suitable sources of fresh meat. The kennel owner should always be prepared to do some cooking for the boarders in case of necessity. However, the time- and labour-saving method is to use a commercially prepared food, or foods from reputable manufacturers.

Several very well-known pet food manufacturers have spent millions of pounds in researching their products and testing them: from these people come not only excellent pet foods but also much of the research into animal nutrition which means healthier lives for pets. In general it is best to deal with reputable, established manufacturers either directly or through their agents.

It has been proved that dogs' diets do not need to be varied, as so many pet owners feel they should, but that the same food is acceptable day in, day out, and in fact a food regime which has been found suitable should be followed without alteration. Therefore, you may be reassured, or even relieved, to know that once you have decided on a basic menu and routine of feeding you need not change it as long as it is satisfactory in the majority of cases. There may always be the occasional dog or cat which refuses outright to fit into your programme, or at first anyway. In such instances your duty is to the animal, not to your regime. For this reason, in addition to your normal foods you should be prepared with some extras tucked away in a freezer or stored suitably – for example, frozen chicken, chicken mince or rabbit, which must be cooked; tins of sardines or pilchards which are particularly tempting for some cats, and also for finicky dogs; perhaps small tins of rice pudding – the sort of things the pets might have at home. In cases of real difficulty, it might be worth remembering that some pets always finish the custard, and others are given the remains of the cereal and milk at breakfast time. Not part of the standard boarding kennel fare but very much part of home life, and if a boarder is very disturbed and disinclined to eat, provided there is no other apparent reason for lack of appetite, it is worth trying a few home treats in the hope that the pet will adjust to a more normal eating pattern. There is usually no need to panic if a new arrival refuses to eat on the first day.

How will you make your choice when deciding on a basic kennel food? It will be wise to consider the various types of dog and cat foods which are produced commercially in a ready-to-serve form, remembering that dogs tend to be omnivorous in their feeding habits but that cats are obligate carnivores. In short, cats *must* have meat in their diets; dogs may prefer meat but can make good nutritional use of other forms of protein including vegetable protein.

Commercially prepared pet foods fall into three main categories.

Canned food

The one most generally known to pet owners is canned pet food, which is preserved by heat sterilisation and therefore does not present the salmonella risks of fresh meat. It keeps in good condition for a long time. It contains a considerable proportion of water and although some canned food is labelled as being a complete diet, because cereal has been added, others may need to be mixed with soaked or dry biscuit meal to make a nutritionally complete meal for dogs. Canned meat for cats is nutritionally complete as it is and may be served without any additions. Most pets are used to a canned food diet; these foods are palatable and, if used correctly, easily digestible. The problems are the time it takes to open numbers of tins, and the disposal problem once they are empty although we are now urged to recycle them.

Semi-moist food

The second type of commercially prepared pet food is known as 'semi-moist'. It is usually sold in packets, often containing inner packs of individual portions, and may have the appearance of mince or meat chunks. It is obviously not the real thing, but the dogs and cats do not seem to mind the rather plastic appearance of the food which is prevented from spoiling by the addition of humectants and mould inhibitors. Semi-moist foods are readily available in the UK for dogs and cats, and such foods are complete and need no supplementation.

Complete dry food

The third type of commercial pet food is known as 'complete dry food'. These foods are cereal based with the addition of meat and fish meal and contain no water. The cheapest ones may be presented in flaky form as the processing is less complicated, but these are sometimes not fully digested. Some complete food may come in a very hard pellet form which some dogs, particularly the smaller breeds, appear to find much too tough and obviously do not care for. Another presentation is an expanded, crunchy pellet form which most dogs enjoy. There are also complete dry foods for cats but these have been, and to a certain extent still are, somewhat controversial. A pet which is fed on dry foods needs to drink more water than if it is fed on canned or semi-moist products; cats may not drink enough water and thus become susceptible to urological problems.

Complete foods for pets are nutritionally balanced and may form the sole diet of the dog or cat, with the proviso that boarding catteries must never use a complete dry food as the *sole* food for cats if the cats are not used to it. Such diets include vitamin and mineral supplements, so additions are unnecessary. Under the Feeding Stuffs Regulations Act 1982, the contents of pet foods, whether complete or complementary, must be listed in descending order of the quantity of the ingredients included in the mixture, and an analysis of the protein, oil, fibre and ash content must be shown.

Pet foods are now being labelled as 'complete' or 'complementary'. A food labelled as a complementary product is not in itself nutritionally complete. Thus a can of dog food indicated as being complementary will need to be served with a biscuit mixer meal, which is also a complementary product, as biscuit mixer served alone would not provide a nutritionally balanced meal either.

The mixer meals, a title which was probably invented to remind users they must be mixed with a meat product to balance the meal, are available in a variety of forms from a very fine puppy grade wholemeal biscuit meal to much larger biscuit chunks suited to larger dogs. Complementary meat products for dogs may be mixed on a half-and-half basis with mixer meals to form the complete nutritional repast. Mixer meals may be soaked in hot water or broth – never use boiling liquid – before being mixed with the meat product. Home products, such as stale wholemeal bread or boiled rice, are also complementary 'mixers' and may be used with meat or fish, fresh or canned.

Vacuum packed meats

As an alternative to canned meat products for dogs there are several brands of vacuum packed meats presented in plastic, sausage-like coverings. These are cooked, minced foods and the dogs find them extremely palatable. 'Chubs' is the name given to the sausage packs, though some also are packed in blocks; such packs have certain advantages in that they are easy to open and the wrappings will not fill the garbage cans to overflowing. Chub packs are claimed by their manufacturers to have a good shelf life, but shorter than the shelf life of canned foods. Chubs and vacuum packs in general do not have to be refrigerated before use, but any leftover meat will need to be. These foods are also complementary and should be served with a biscuit mixer. However, new dog foods, or the same types of food in different packs, are continually coming on to the market and before using any pet food the kennel owner should check the list of contents and directions for use.

Deep frozen food

Other types of dog food are the deep frozen products. These may have been cooked and then deep frozen; some are frozen raw and thus need cooking. In either case the water content is quite high and it is necessary to have freezer space for storage, and a good memory so that the frozen blocks are left out to thaw. It is probably useful to have some of these products in the freezer even though it may not be practical to use frozen foods for the entire kennel at all times. Again, frozen foods are complementary products and need a biscuit mixer to complete the menu. Usually, dogs find frozen foods palatable, after they are thoroughly cooked, of course.

Boil-in-the-bag food

A further method of packing pet foods is in 'boil-in-the-bag' containers, and though these may be favoured by some pet owners they are not practical for boarding kennel use except, of course, as a tempting starter for a reluctant feeder.

Fresh, canned, vacuum packed, deep frozen or boil-in-the-bag meat or fish products for pets which need to be served with a mixer meal are more expensive to use than either the semi-moist complete foods or the complete dry foods, even though boarding kennel owners with large orders may buy in bulk. They are also more time- and labour-consuming and for these reasons many boarding kennels use complete dry foods for *dogs*; complete canned diets, or fresh foods, are the most suitable for *cats* in the boarding environment, although cats which are used to it may relish a small percentage of dry cat food.

Tripe

Readers with some experience of dog care will wonder why tripe has not been mentioned among the suitable foods for dogs. Some breeding kennels use tripe which is satisfactory in protein and fat content but is deficient in minerals. Also, it is not cost-effective.

Tripe at its best is purchased direct from an abattoir. This smelly, messy purchase then has to be cleaned, cut and frozen. Unprocessed, it attracts flies. Prepacked, cut or minced tripe can be bought from bulk suppliers, but this is much more expensive and needs freezer space. It is very smelly when defrosting. Tripe can be cooked although dogs love it raw; some people insist it should be cooked. Try that and even the dogs may want to leave the premises, not to mention what the neighbours might say. Tripe used consistently in a kennel creates a strong smell which your clients will be quick to notice. It is one ingredient of most manufactured canned, frozen or vacuum packed meat foods for dogs, so let them enjoy it in that more innocuous form. Tripe is not a complete food and must be used with a mixer meal.

The use of complete dry diets for dogs and cats

Not a great many pet dogs are fed by their owners on complete dry foods. There are two reasons for this: the non-availability of small packs where most pet owners do their shopping – the local supermarket – and the refusal of pet owners to believe that a product which looks like a form of canine breakfast cereal is in fact a complete diet. Conversely, cat owners are more likely to have used some complete dry cat food though its use is somewhat controversial! Here the reason is that the complete dry cat foods tend to be packed in smaller amounts, possibly because cats are smaller animals; supermarkets are therefore able to display the products more easily, and dry foods for cats receive a great deal of advertising on television.

When deciding to use a complete dry food as a basic kennel diet it is necessary to remember two most important factors. First, as most pet dogs will not be used to such foods they need to be introduced to it gradually, served with a meat product at first, then reducing the meat as the dry food is accepted. Second, dry feeding makes the pet more thirsty, so extra attention must be paid to refilling water bowls and checking that fresh drinking water is always available to each boarder. Particular care must be taken with dogs which continually spill their water bowls, or paddle in them, as some delight in doing. Dry foods can, of course, be fed pre-soaked though most dogs seem to prefer them to be crunchy rather than mushy.

Dry feeding has proved to be not only the most convenient but also the most economical and nutritionally satisfactory method of feeding dogs in any environment. Carefully chosen and correctly used dry foods are suitable for all dogs from the puppy to the geriatric stage. Therefore, once a dry complete food has been chosen it can be used as a basic food throughout the entire dog kennel. How will you make your choice of a complete dry food? There are basically three different types, all nutritionally complete. Which is most suited to your kennel requirements? If your choice is governed by price, there is sufficient variation in dry feeding costs to allow for individual choice, and availability of the product must also play a part in the decision. Advertisements for most complete dry foods can be found in the weekly dog papers; the manufacturers' representatives can be seen at championship dog shows, or you can write to the manufacturers for a price-list and the name of the nearest agent, or enquire whether the manufacturer will supply you direct.

In dry dog foods, meat and fish meals are added to cooked cereals which are further supplemented with vitamin and mineral additives. The manufacturing method controls the price of these foods, and also the protein content, thus the overall nutritional value.

Dogs, unlike cats, do not require a high protein diet containing a large proportion of meat. Complete dry foods vary in protein content from about 18 to around 30 per cent. The higher protein content foods are required for bitches in whelp and puppy rearing, and the middle range is nutritionally very suitable for most dogs. Dogs digest cooked cereals well, and also fat from which they get their energy requirements. Vegetables are not important for dogs as they do not require vitamin C. Cereal products also supply fibre and this leads to the formation of a firm stool – a welcome attribute in the boarding kennel environment as cleaning is made easier.

Some complete dry foods may be presented as loose meals, or flaky foods which tend to be low in fat content and are a simple mix of the required ingredients. The flaked cereals are cooked as a rule, and this makes them more digestible. They are best served soaked or mixed with a gravy, and are ready for serving immediately. Many dogs do not find these meals altogether palatable or digestible, so some meat may be added to make them readily acceptable. Brands such as Vitalin, Royal Canin and Roberts & Co's 'Natural 19' have been available for many years, and there are several others. These foods tend to deteriorate more quickly in storage than other dry foods, but in the boarding kennel environment this is less likely to be a problem as the food turnover is rapid. However, any dry foods you purchase should have a datemark on them: either a date of manufacture, or a 'use by' date.

A second type of dry dog food is pelleted, rather like cattle or pony cubes. These foods tend to be very hard and may be refused by smaller breeds. They do not soak well and usually are less popular, particularly when there are all sizes and ages of dogs to consider. They are also more expensive than the flaky meals.

The most popular type of dry complete diet is the expanded meal. This has a porous texture and the pellets are coated with fat, some brands having a higher oil content than others, though none looks fatty or is greasy to the touch. This meal absorbs liquid easily; therefore expanded meals soak well for the dogs which like a soft mash, and are crispy and crunchy for those which prefer a hard chew.

Though expanded meals are more palatable than either the flaky foods or the rock-hard pellets, nothing is so tasty to a dog as meat. Therefore, while the dog is getting used to his new food the addition of a small amount of canned meat to the expanded meal will help a great deal. Many dogs in breeding kennels are fed on expanded meals and this works well in the boarding kennel too.

Dry, crunchy diets are also good for the dogs' teeth and gums, but do be careful about topping up those water bowls! A few well known examples of expanded meals are Iams Eukanuba, Omega, Spratts Dog Diet, Wafcol, Beta and Go Dog. The manufacturers supply their expanded complete diets with different protein contents and in some cases in different size pellets to cater for all sizes and types of dogs, of all ages and stages of growth and development. Because of the higher protein content of expanded meals – 24 to 30 per cent approximately – a dog needs less of this type of food than if it were fed on the next most popular diet, a half meat and half mixer meal dinner. See the table on page 88 which give a guide to the food intake requirements of dogs.

The great advantages of complete dry foods are their safety factors: they are nutritious for the pets, very easy and clean to serve, do not attract flies and carry no salmonella risks.

Daily amount of food

Weight of dog lb	Approx energy need kcal	Mixed diet Meal oz	+ Meat oz	Expanded meal oz
10	425	3½	+3½	4½
20	700	5½	+5½	7½
30	950	7½	+7½	10
40	1200	9½	+9½	12½
50	1400	11	+11	14½
60	1600	13	+13	16½
70	1800	14½	+14½	18½
80	1950	15½	+15½	20½
90	2100	16½	+16½	22
100	2250	18	+18	23½

Reproduced by kind permission of Dr Alan Walker and *Kennel and Cattery Management* magazine.

Self-feeding

Sometimes called hopper feeding, this method of feeding the boarders is looked on as the ultimate in time-saving. Another name for the practice is *ad lib* feeding. Whatever the name used, it consists of filling a hopper or other vessel with a day's supply of dry food for each dog and the feeding chores are done. This method is suitable for use with dry foods because they do not attract flies. Naturally, an adequate water supply also has to be arranged and there are various self-fill drinkers which might be used.

In theory, the dog helps itself to as much food as it wants, when it wants it. The chief disadvantage to *ad lib* feeding is that a great many dogs are greedy and wolf the whole lot at once, which may be quite a shock to the dog's digestive organs. Others scatter the food and play with it. For some boarders the system may work well, but as a rule it is not much favoured in the UK though it is mentioned more often in the USA kennel guides.

An argument against this method of feeding is that pets arriving at your kennel will have come from homes where they are in constant contact with people. They come into what they may look on as a prison, a confined space without the presence of their own humans. The mechanisation of the feeding chores, if mechanisation is not too strong a word, tends to remove another human contact and may not be conducive to easy settling in a strange environment. Furthermore, if two or more dogs from the same household are kennelled together who will know what dog ate which portion? *Ad lib* feeding has its disadvantages.

Conclusion

Expert surveys have shown that the most economical method of feeding dogs overall is to use an expanded complete meal as a basic kennel feed. It would be extremely wrong to suggest that there should be any 'basic' feed in a cattery, as cats are totally individual and selective in all things.

Economy, though necessary, should not be the overriding factor. The food must be palatable. If the boarders do not like the food they will not eat it. If the food is not nutritionally adequate and satisfying they will lose weight and you will have to give them more food – or be accused of starving them! Labour costs and regular food supplies must be considered; it is a nightmare for owners when deliveries are delayed by bad weather or strikes. Obtain all the information you can about the food you think you might like to use in your kennels and find out how to obtain it at the most reasonable prices.

Think carefully about your feeding plans. They play a major part in your care of the boarders. Well chosen products used to their best advantage can help you over some of the difficulties which, before your initiation as a boarding kennel owner, you may not have realised existed.

Chapter 8

The Daily Round

Everyday work in a boarding kennel begins early and goes on until it is finished. Much of the work is done during what, in other occupations, are usually called 'unsocial hours'. If you employ staff they will obviously have set hours. The owners sometimes wonder if they will ever have any time to themselves, particularly in the busy season.

The daily work falls roughly into two major categories which overlap: the first concerns the care of the boarders, keeping their accommodation clean and hygienic, seeing they have exercise and good food and are comfortable and happy; the second concerns the kennel's public face, relationships between the kennel and its human clients, between owner and staff, between the kennel and those who supply its material needs and who give their professional services.

Your clients should be informed through your advertising, brochures, booking application forms and by the largest, clearest sign you can possibly erect at your kennel entrance, exactly what hours the kennel is open for business. Or, to put it another way, when your kennel is definitely, absolutely, irrevocably *closed* for business! Because you 'live over the shop', so to speak, clients are often tempted to telephone or visit after normal business hours; it is necessary to guard your privacy – first, because you deserve some time off duty during which you are unavailable to callers, and second, because visitors disturb the dogs and send them into a frenzy of barking, and after hours disturbances should be avoided if possible. There may be occasions when for a good reason a dog or cat may have to be collected after your official closing time; provided you are given notice of this, arrangements can be made to bring the pet down to the reception area, or to a handy kennel which will not involve disturbing a whole building.

Exercise

Pets are used to being let out first thing in the morning so that is the first task. Let out where? If each kennel has its own attached run, the dogs can be let into their runs while their kennels are cleaned and disinfected, and allowed to return for a biscuit snack or a morning meal if their feeding plan is so arranged.

When kennels do not have their own attached runs it is necessary to take each dog individually to an outside run, and if the weather is wet the dog still has to go out and be dried when it is brought back to its clean kennel. In such establishments it is more helpful if there are a number of medium-sized outdoor exercise runs, all safely fenced of course, rather than one larger area. Dogs should not be mixed together unless they come from the same household; the same applies to cats – those from the same home may share a chalet, otherwise each cat has its own individual unit. Mixing pets from various households is an invitation to fights, something to be avoided at all costs.

Another early morning job, and one which may have to be repeated at suitable intervals throughout the day, is to give special consideration to the new boarders who may be so well house-trained that they will neither soil their kennel nor perform their toilet functions in the attached run. Such dogs are probably used to the unrestricted use of their gardens at home, or will not foul their own property at all but 'perform' only when taken for walks. Such dogs may respond well to free running in a grass enclosure, in the absence of which it may be necessary to lead-walk the dog. Unfortunately, some pet owners train their dogs rather too well, not understanding that training can be overdone.

Some boarding kennel owners report that cats who have not been used to using a litter tray at home do not take too kindly to one in a kennel. In such cases the problem might be solved by adding some clean earth to the litter tray until the cat has got the message. Needless to say, cat litter trays must be cleaned and disinfected every day.

Cleaning routine

The subject of kennel cleaning has been dealt with in Chapter 6 but as a subject of prime importance it cannot be too heavily emphasised. The basic directions are to clean first, then disinfect using a kennel disinfectant preparation in the exact quantities recommended by the manufacturers. Proper kennel disinfectants are expensive, but necessary; check the dilutions are measured correctly, not just casually tipped into a bucket.

Though cat boarders are not allowed out of their runs during their stay with you they too must have their chalets opened each morning and cleaned meticulously according to the recommendations of the Feline Advisory Bureau (see Chapter 6). Cats should always be shut into their chalets at night, with their sanitary tray, and the cat flap secured.

Cleaning includes the proper washing and sterilisation of feeding and drinking bowls. The most intensive floor, wall and run cleaning will be of little use if feeding and drinking vessels are infection carriers; there are special sterilising detergents for these utensils. For cats it may be considered better to use disposable feeding dishes, remembering that many disinfectants are toxic to them. Disposable feeding dishes can be incinerated.

It is useful to have some disinfectant sprays handy in the kennel and cattery. Tego is excellent used in a spray container and is recommended by the Feline Advisory Bureau. Kennel folk can use these sprays to clean their hands after cleaning up vomit or handling a dirty animal. The spray quickly deals with soiled hands and helps to prevent the spread of infection. Small plant misters are ideal for this use.

Newspaper is a very useful commodity in daily use in some kennels and most pets are used to it at home. Not the least of your daily tasks is the disposal of excrement and other kennel rubbish. This has been referred to fully in Chapter 6, but make sure that this is tackled promptly and correctly. There is no worse advertisement for your kennel than to show visitors around uncleaned kennels and runs.

Mealtimes

When the morning cleaning, tidying and exercising is completed the boarders may relish either a snack or a meal; it all depends on your catering schedule. Some kennels prefer to serve the main meal in the morning, others in the late afternoon; some owners even prefer to feed the dogs in the late evening; others may decide to feed the dogs two meals a day. When the main meal is planned is not so important as the fact that it is served at the same time every day. A fact which may affect the timing of the dogs' main meal is whether it will be served by you, or your staff. Staff work set hours, and anyone who is off duty at 5 pm is not the person to serve the dogs' main meal at 4.30. It used to be the rule in breeding kennels to fast the dogs on one day each week – this was normally Sunday, the kennel maid's day off! Pet dogs are not used to fasting on one day each week, so regardless of staff problems the dogs are fed one or two meals a day, and cats are fed twice each day.

The approach of feeding time in a dog kennel is noisy. The clatter of food bowls is enough to indicate that a meal is on the way, and joyous anticipatory barking begins. Fortunately, the post-prandial time is quiet and dogs should be allowed to rest after they have eaten. This is when you will need a break too, so make the most of it. Many kennels follow a practice called 'feeding in', which basically means that the dog is brought into its kennel, access to the run is closed, dinner is served and eaten, and only after a rest period is the dog let out again. This prevents the dogs charging around their runs in excitement should something interesting happen right after mealtime, which is not good for the digestion. When they are let out after their rest the feeding bowls can be collected, washed and sterilised. This is the time to note whether any of the boarders have not eaten their food. Unless a quiet and undisturbed period follows immediately after the food is served the poor or slow eaters may simply be too interested in whatever else is going on and forget they are supposed to be having dinner. Non-eaters should be so indicated on their health charts (see pages 94–95).

The kennel kitchen

The kennel kitchen is a very important part of the property. Separate kitchen departments in each kennel block assist in preventing the spread of any infection. Many boarding kennels have a central dog kitchen and, wherever the kitchen is situated, the overriding need is for it to be spotlessly clean and checked daily for hygiene and adequate supplies. A note should be made of any products which need to be reordered, and loose meals should be stored in vermin-proof containers. Regardless of whether the basic kennel menu needs any cooking there should be cooking facilities for special cases and also a refrigerator and a freezer. Such appliances are often available at nominal prices from second-hand shops or auctions but check that they are in working order before you buy. A washing machine, again a second-hand bargain would do, is a most useful item.

Every kitchen needs a good sink of sufficient size, plus hot and cold water. Those feeding bowls and drinking dishes need to be washed and sterilised and, though the future may bring more automation to this kennel task, the present-day kennel which has even a second-hand automatic dishwasher is in the five star class. People seeking kennel properties to start their own business frequently report abysmally inadequate kitchen facilities and equipment. Far too many do not even have a hot water supply, yet these places are inspected and apparently found adequate as the licences are renewed.

Having prepared the boarders' food there is the business of taking the meals to the dogs and cats. In a block of a dozen kennels which has its own kitchen, serving 12 bowls of dinner will not be a daunting task. In a central kitchen serving 60 or 70 meals the distribution of the food from the kitchen to the eagerly awaiting consumer would tax the ingenuity of an experienced waiter. Some method of transporting as many meals as possible on one journey has to be devised. A trolley seems to be the ideal solution. A water carrier on the trolley allows drinking bowls to be replenished at the same time. Time- and labour-saving devices may be inventions of your own or adapted from other people's ideas. When you look around kennels, note good ideas which you may find useful, or on which you can improve.

Beds and towels

The dogs' bedding needs checking every day. It is usually best if the boarders bring their own beds and bedding with them as a reminder of home. Strangely enough the pets may decide to while away their happy holiday hours in destroying their beds. When a destructive period seems to be approaching it is best to remove the pet's own bedding and substitute some kennel supplies. Alternatively, there are many dogs which, despite their owners having brought their bed and bedding, will prefer to sprawl on the floor of the kennel. For big dogs it is useful to have a large raised bench so they can be encouraged to get up off the floor, preferably on to a blanket. Some large dogs, Great Danes for example, have thin coats and can acquire pressure sores from lying on concrete. Sheets of corrugated cardboard may help 'soften' a hard floor; sometimes carpet firms will donate out-of-date samples to you. All such items, after use as bedding, should be destroyed when the boarder returns home.

Some kennels advertise that they provide 'jumble bedding' – a totally off-putting thought. However, some bedding must be produced. Jameson Veterinary Fleece, a very hard-wearing and comfortable synthetic fur fabric, makes hygienic, washable bedding for dogs and cats. One of its assets is that it does not retain moisture and therefore dries quickly. Blankets are also useful, and special blankets for kennel use may be obtained from Leonard's of Downton, Wiltshire or the Bedding Box, Abersychan, Pontypool, Gwent.

Towels are another necessity for use in kennels, but at present there seems to be no specialist supplier of towels for kennel use. Household towels which are past their best usually find their way to the kennel stores; perhaps jumble sales might be another possible source, or auction sales or army surplus sales. One possible solution is to ask the boarders' owners to bring their pets' towels with them but be sure to send towels home clean! Small dogs with very long coats, Shih Tzu, Lhasa Apsos, Long-haired Dachsunds, Yorkshire Terriers, Pekinese and similar little dogs can act like wet mops on a rainy day, and must not be allowed to stay wet. A professional electric dog dryer is a great asset in a boarding kennel.

Taking stock

Each day a check needs to be made on the stock of cleaning materials and foodstuffs. Allow time for reordering and delivery, and then allow more time for unexpected delays! Another daily check involves close inspection of run fencing, kennels and cat chalets with a view to possible damage and the need for repairs. Never leave a gate or fence unrepaired. You will undoubtedly be surprised by the damage that may be inflicted by one small pet, or how some dogs can climb chain link fencing, bite through wire netting and generally create chaos. Large dogs simply do a better job more quickly! Latches, hinges, locks, check them all. Some dogs and cats practically vandalise their accommodation, necessitating ultra careful cleaning and repairs.

Heating

A daily check on heating is essential in the interest of comfort and economy. When you take over a boarding kennel or build a new one, you will have little idea at first of the temperature variation within the building. Invest in some maximum-minimum thermometers such as are used in greenhouses. Then keep a note of the highest and lowest temperatures; it will help you to assess heating needs, or in the hottest months show you the degree of heat you and the boarders have to endure. Insulation in kennel building can vary from quite good to non-existent: it affects the running costs of heating appliances in proportion to its effectiveness.

Health record cards

Each boarder should have its own health record card updated daily while it stays with you. Even in a small kennel it is no use relying solely on your memory of what has happened during the course of each day. The boarder's health card can be hung in its kennel, out of reach of the pet, and should record basic details such as normal bowel movements, or otherwise, diarrhoea, constipation, vomiting, lameness, runny eyes, a cough, whether a bitch is in season, or anything which seems unusual. Cats are more inclined to suffer in silence and particular care should be paid to them. Whether or not the cat is eating should be noted, also if a cat has difficulty in urinating; this situation may need prompt veterinary attention. The owner should check the pet's health records daily and, if there is any concern, request a visit from the vet. Therefore, do not leave the daily health check until late afternoon; vets are busy people too and have to plan their rounds. Without a written health record it would be difficult to answer the basic questions the vet will have to ask in order to help in diagnosis.

A continuity of care is essential in the boarding kennel and cattery, and as the same staff may not be on duty all the time the health cards provide that essential continuity. Record cards can be designed to suit your own needs, just as long as you and your staff understand your system and use it correctly.

Grooming

Dogs and cats in boarding kennels should be groomed regularly, and particularly before leaving. Whether you offer only simple basic grooming (that is, brushing and combing with a good quality coat spray dressing), or whether you have a trained canine beautician and can therefore offer full bathing, grooming and trimming facilities for all breeds, is a matter you should make clear to your clients. The basic brushing, combing and tidying with the help of a pleasant-smelling coat dressing should be part of the normal service. The full, professional treatment is an extra. However, no dog should leave your kennels looking unkempt. Check carefully the coats of all long, or heavy coated breeds which may board with you. It is quite likely that you will find many are badly matted, and if you do not offer a full grooming service you should suggest that the dogs should be taken to a professional beautician, preferably a member of the Groomers Association, for the correct coat treatment. A matted dog is often a miserable dog, and very uncomfortable.

Reception area

The daily round will bring visitors to your kennel: people bringing or collecting boarders, merchandise deliverymen, people who wish to inspect your kennels before making a firm booking, local government officials inspecting your kennels under statutory regulations and almost anybody you are prepared to admit. Visitors will interest the dogs if they can see them arrive, or if they can watch the cars come and go. Dogs show their interest with a vocal greeting. If your visitors' arrivals and your reception area can be screened from the boarders' view so much the better, and if visitors are restricted to your official opening hours the dogs should be quieter in the evenings. Prospective clients who want to look around the kennels should be invited at certain times only, and adults rather than children encouraged. Of course, people should see where their pets are going to stay but you are not providing kennel tours for fun, so plan these visits for midweek if possible. At the weekends you are likely to be extra busy and possibly short of staff.

Security dictates that entrance to your kennel should be on admittance by one of the staff. People arriving need to know what to do; place a notice on the gate asking visitors to ring the bell and wait, but make sure the bell is connected and answered without delay. There is nothing more demoralising for a person who may be rather reluctantly boarding a pet than to arrive at your kennel and find nobody waiting with a friendly word of welcome. It also gives a very poor impression of your kennel's security! The sign reading, 'RECEPTION. PLEASE RING AND WAIT' is a much better start.

The reception room may also be the kennel office. It is advisable to keep all the bookwork in one place or you will be forever wanting to refer to something which is in another place when needed. How you organise your office work may depend on whether you or your partner have any experience of secretarial work, or whether you are going to employ some part-time clerical help. Under the Animal Boarding Establishments Act 1963 you are bound to keep a register of the animals boarded with you. Keep your boarders' register in your reception area; basically, it should show which dogs are in which kennels, when they arrived and when they are expected to depart. Advance bookings can be entered in pencil until confirmation and a deposit is received; then the booking can be inked in. Never overbook the accommodation as there is always the possibility that an owner may be quite legitimately delayed and unable to collect a pet on time.

You will also need a file in which to keep the booking forms which are a business contract between you and the pet owner. Booking forms should always be issued in duplicate; one copy for your file, and the other copy for the pet owner – both copies showing clear signatures. Your kennel stationery and brochures need to be in your office/reception room, also the typewriter or computer if you have one and, as you will be taking money, a lockable compartment or safe, depending on the size of your business and what valuables must be secured. The reception office should be clean, neat and comfortable in its own way, and as attractive as possible as this will be your clients' first introduction to your premises. There should be a spare cat-carrying basket in case someone arrives with puss loose in the car. A large dog crate is also a useful item to have handy, and some spare slip leads. The reception area should look efficient and inviting. Shabby paint and an air of dilapidation can be remedied fairly easily, and a few doggy pictures, prize rosettes, or even attractive pot plants give a welcoming appearance.

The telephone should be in the office, though you may have extensions at other strategic points. Consider one of the modern telephone answering aids to ease the burden of phone calls but beware of the machine that broadcasts a recorded message: people simply do not like them. Consult the telephone company for details of the cordless telephones which can be carried around with you, or if you feel that the answering machine has to be your choice, make a polite recording with the dogs barking in the background – it leaves nobody in doubt that dogs are around!

One very important item which should be kept in your reception office and updated each year is a list of canine breed rescue societies and the names of the people responsible for administering them for each breed. The list is sponsored by *Our Dogs* and Pedigree Petfoods and is complied by Mrs Sheila Alcock, telephone 01438 871288. If owners of uncollected boarders are impossible to trace after a period, the kennel owner usually tries to re-home a healthy animal and often the breed rescue society can help. Alternatively, if a client mentions that he or she is hoping to find another home for the dog, the kennel owners may put the person in touch with the breed rescue society direct and save themselves a headache! Another address to note is that of the Cats Protection League, 20 North Street, Horsham, West Sussex RH12 1BN.

If you are interested in computers for the small business, investigate the possibilities. Some large quarantine kennels and wholesale dog food businesses use computers for some aspects of the business, and many more boarding kennels now rely on computers or PCWS.

Arrivals and departures

When new boarders arrive, check their booking forms with the owners and note that they have been signed by them and by you, or by someone signing with your authority. Confirm that the pet owners understand the terms of boarding and check carefully the pets' vaccination certificates. *No boarder can be admitted without a current vaccination certificate.* This is not only sensible on your part but is a requirement of many local councils. Make sure you have the owner's correct address and a contact with whom you can get in touch if necessary, and check that the owners know exactly when they are due to collect their pets.

New boarders must be seen safely to their holiday kennel or chalet. It is easier for you to use your own leads. Strong nylon slip leads are easy to use and can be carried in your pocket. Choke chains should be used with care and assistants instructed in their correct use. Cats should be taken to their chalets in their baskets and not released until they are safely within their own enclosure. Remind kennel staff to be just as welcoming to the pets as they are to the owners, and to be prepared to give the new arrivals a little extra attention to help them settle down.

Of course, no dog leaves your boarding kennel unless the bill is paid in full. No money, no pet. Bank cards guarantee cheques up to £50. Over that amount, it is trust or cash. At the departure stage it will be a great relief to all concerned if no unexpected extras are added to the bill; a charge for veterinary treatment is one possibility, but that may never occur if your kennels are fully covered by insurance with one of the major canine insurance companies.

Another facet of the daily round is whether or not you will collect or deliver boarders. There are two major considerations here. People should always see where their pets are going to stay, which means they should visit your kennels, and collecting and delivering take time – time is money and there are petrol costs and the wear and tear on your car or van. It is better if the owners of the pets do the fetching and carrying, but there will be some instances when flexibility in this matter will pay dividends. Somebody's car has broken down, perhaps, or some other hitch in the plans makes it impossible for them to transport Rover to your kennels. Help them out; make a charge or, in certain cases, you may be prepared to waive the collection charge. Use your discretion.

Enquiries ~~New Read Read Read~~

Almost every day prospective clients, or other inquisitive folk, telephone to ask how much you charge to board dogs or cats. Try to work out a plan for answering such calls, and train your staff to use whatever method you have worked out. The boarding kennel owner has to be his own salesman, and though he can hardly put his foot in the door he can perhaps prevent a caller ringing off before some useful, attractive and enticing information has been passed along the line. It takes only a few seconds to give some information, or obtain some, *before* you tell the price! Answer the question, 'How much do you charge?' with 'What sort of dog/cat do you have?' Whatever size, breed, etc is mentioned will be your favourite, and you have exactly the right accommodation for them. Of course you will go on to say that your prices are inclusive of all the pets' needs, heating, insurance and, if necessary, veterinary fees. In short you are offering absolutely super value in ideal surroundings at £X per day or whatever the relevant fee may be. There is nothing wrong with a good line of salesmanship, the point of which is to instil confidence in the mind of the caller and, without saying so, make it quite clear that the cheapest is not always the best. You are running a business which must be profitable despite the weird ideas that some people have about it being not quite the thing to make money out of a doggy pursuit. You are offering a service – a good one; if it does not pay, the service is lost to the neighbourhood and your business is lost too.

Problems which may be encountered

Aged pets

Old age canines and felines may sometimes have to become boarders. If they have not been regularly boarded over the years it may be a very great shock to them and have the direst consequences. Warn the owners that it is a terrible strain on the older dog or cat and show these boarders every attention and extra comfort – which may include smaller meals more often – and the quietest kennel available so that the dog will not be disturbed too much. Conversely, the aged feline may relish its own secluded chalet, with all its needs cared for, meals-on-wheels, and extra fuss, and be very content. If an elderly boarder is having any medicines, make sure you have an adequate supply for its stay with you, and be sure to give the drugs as directed.

Bitches in season
Always ask the pet owners if a bitch is spayed, or when it is due in season. If a bitch has not been spayed it is quite likely that the experience of coming into the boarding kennel may bring her into season, or she may already be on heat and that is why her owners have boarded her with you. A bitch in season will delight, tease and annoy the dogs, even though she does nothing special to attract their attention. The boys will *know*! Put her in a kennel and run which does not have a male neighbour on either side. Remember that a determined male can be a Houdini plus and will attempt to join her. Secure, covered runs help a great deal, but accidental marriages have occurred. Should you be so lax you must stand the cost of the annulment: an injection given by the vet. A disadvantage of bitches in season is that the dogs love to serenade them, preferably about 1 am.

Fights
To be avoided at all costs. Make it clear to your clients that all dogs arrive at the kennels on a lead, and that cats are securely shut into their baskets or cat carriers. Cats are not let out of their carriers until safely within their own quarters with the run door firmly closed. Dogs are moved from A to B within the kennel on a lead and only pets from the same household are allowed to be kennelled together or play together in an exercise run. A dog in the boarding environment, though quite amiable and docile, may be cherishing a desire to have a go at its neighbour or the dog up the corridor, and once the opportunity for a punch-up occurs the results can be serious; in such circumstances the human is very likely to be bitten and the dogs may bite each other badly too. Do *not* let fights start.

Fleas
Some boarding kennels make it a practice to spray every new boarder on arrival with Nuvantop or one of the other prescribed flea killers, just to be on the safe side. If you have the facilities and the expertise for bathing and grooming, a flea bath could well be indicated: use a veterinary prescribed shampoo such as Quellada or Derasect or one recommended by your vet.

Kennel cough

Any coughing dog should be considered with suspicion, as kennel cough is very infectious and by the time you have heard the first coughs and splutters the dog will have passed it on to most of his fellow boarders. Some dogs are not severely affected by kennel cough, though it makes others very ill. Those most susceptible are the very young and the very old, or any dog whose health is somewhat below par. The outbreak may start with a dog which was perfectly well when it arrived but was incubating the disease; other dogs may go home apparently well and start coughing in a day or two. Veterinary advice should be sought as there may be secondary problems; antibiotics and a cough syrup may be prescribed. Remember that dogs which have recovered from kennel cough remain infectious for several months, so suggest that your clients consult their vet regarding protection with Intrac nasal vaccine before boarding.

Medicines

The kennel owner, or a person of responsibility and experience only, should administer prescribed medicine according to instructions, and each dose should be recorded on the pet's health record card. This is not a job for junior staff or part-timers. A tranquilliser which calms down one dog may not affect the next. A pill which has no effect on a small dog may knock out a larger breed for many hours. Tolerance of tranquillisers and certain other drugs appears to vary, not only with the size of the dog but also with the breed. Not all dogs react alike to medicines.

Worms

It is possible that you may see round worms, which look like thin spaghetti, or even tapeworm segments, which look like particles of long grain rice, in a dog's motions or in the anal area. If so, do not rush in with the worm medicine until you have checked with your vet that you have the right anthelmintic (worm medicine). Should a cat produce worms *do not* use your dog worming medicine! Cat medicines are not the same as dog medicines. Follow the directions carefully.

Tail damage

A large dog with a very waggy tail may damage its tail tip against kennel walls or run partitions; then every wag sprays a shower of blood spots which inevitably worries the dog's owner, the kennel owner and the staff far more than it bothers the dog. Tail damage of this sort is to be avoided if possible. A very excitable dog which likes to jump up with a woof and a wag at every opportunity may be calmed down if it is put in a quieter kennel where it cannot see quite so much of what is going on. Never resort to tranquillisers without specific advice.

Post mortems

If one of your boarders dies while in your care, an event one always hopes will not happen but which unfortunately can occur through no fault of yours, your vet should always be asked to ascertain the cause of death. This may involve a post mortem, and certainly will involve your insurance company: another reason why you need proper insurance coverage organised by a specialist company. You cannot afford legal claims for reimbursement, nor ill-will from a bereaved client. For a client to return from a wonderful holiday only to find a beloved pet has died is a truly harrowing experience.

Noise

Last, but by no means least, is the most common kennel problem of all – noise. Noise is the chief reason for complaints against a kennel, and complaints are always worrying. Everything else about your establishment may be perfect but anyone who is annoyed by the barking will not see one good point in your favour.

Your environmental health officer will be the person instructed to visit you if there are complaints of noise, and may well have some helpful suggestions to make for alleviating the problem. Well insulated buildings will deaden the sound of barking from within. Restricting visitors to certain times, not accepting or releasing boarders after 6 pm, feeding late in the afternoon and generally finishing all kennel work by early evening is helpful. The kennel which has visitors coming and going at all hours is bound to provide sufficient disturbances to keep the dogs noisy. Apart from annoying the neighbours, it is not a good idea to allow unwarranted barking; the dogs go home with hoarse voices and sore throats!

Sometimes it is necessary to do some detective work to find out why there is unusual noise. For example, some kennels use infra-red overhead heaters in kennels at night of which there are two types: one gives a warm red glow of light as well as heat, and the other is known as a dull emitter and gives comforting warmth but no light. Use only the dull emitter type of infra-red heater or the pet may wake up and bark because somebody has left the light on! They feel disorientated, and say so.

Veterinary surgeons' visits

If it is necessary to call a veterinary surgeon to visit a boarder, try to contact the practice as early as possible in the day – a good reason for an early morning health check in the kennel. But illness can occur at any time of the day or night and attention sought as soon as possible is the best plan.

Consider how veterinary examinations can best be carried out at your kennel before the need arises. Will the vet see the patient in its own kennel? Is the kennel big enough? Is it sufficiently well lit to allow a proper examination? Do you have a dispensary, or treatment/grooming room which you could use for such visits? Is there a sink? Is your boarders' first aid box well stocked?

If a cat needs to be examined this is best done in the cat's own chalet. The FAB suggested individual chalet 6 × 4 × 6 ft, has a bench underneath the window and a light, and allows two people to be present while a cat is examined. Penthouse cat accommodation is quite difficult in such circumstances, and some forms of cat accommodation are totally inadequate yet somehow they have been licensed. If it is impossible to examine a cat in its own accommodation, moving it may increase the chance of spreading infection.

Isolation

By law you must provide one isolation section for dogs and one for cats if you board both species. It would be extremely cruel to expect an ailing cat to be comfortable and reassured if its isolation quarters were in close proximity to the dogs' sick quarters. For either species the isolation unit must be adequate in size, comfortable, with provision for extra heating – an overhead infra-red dull emitter thermostatically controlled would be suitable – and the units should be in a place where you and your staff can easily give the extra attention which will be needed.

Medication

Finally, if you do not know the easy ways to give medicines to cats or dogs when they are prescribed, ask your vet to show you. Many dogs will take a pill concealed in a piece of meat, hidden in a titbit of cheese or pilchard perhaps. Liquid medicine is easiest given from a syringe; ask your vet for one. Giving a pill to a cat may need a step-by-step lesson from an expert. Have somebody show you and thus avoid some scratches! A few pet animals are 'unpillable'; no matter what ruse you try the pill will not stay down. In such cases the medicine can perhaps be obtained in a liquid form. If medicine cannot be given orally, injection may be the answer. Never give up; if a sick animal requires medication then it is your duty to see that the dose goes in, one way or another, and reducing yourself to a shaking wreck will not help matters.

Final check

The kennel owner's last duty of the day is to make the last round of the kennel property and check that all boarders are in their kennels, or cat units, and appear to be well. Check that all buildings are secure and that the outside runs have been left absolutely clean. Then it is 'lights out' after a busy, satisfying and, hopefully, not too problematical day.

Chapter 9

Kennel Staff

In the early days of your boarding kennel ownership you may find that your kennel can be managed without extra help. A husband/wife team, or two working partners, can usually manage very well in a small business, but the single-handed kennel owner will need some back-up help if only of a part-time nature. There are so many things which only the owner can attend to, and the basic kennel work has to be done regardless of interruptions. Some of the enjoyment of being your own boss begins to wear thin if you are constantly overtired through attending single-handed to all the cleaning, maintenance, bookwork and queries from clients, prospective clients and officials of one sort or another.

Before employing help, decide if kennel help is what you need; that is, do you need help with the actual care of the kennels and the dogs and cats? You might find that you and your partner are very happy doing everything in the animal departments but that outside help with the housework, garden, children or secretarial work is what you really want. Kennel work is demanding and strenuous and therefore meals need to be more than a rushed snack when you can get around to it, or a take-away evening meal from whatever local source is available. You will need time out to visit the dentist, have a hair-cut or attend to any of the small necessities of life. Perhaps regular full- or part-time help is needed, but not actually with the animals. Boarding kennel owners who are also active in the dog or cat exhibition world, and wish to remain so, will find that they need experienced help with the boarders as they may have to leave them in charge of an assistant who will have full responsibility in their absence. Ancillary help is one end of the staff spectrum; a kennel manager/manageress is at the other. Determine your own particular needs and also what you can afford to pay. There is sure to be a going rate for domestic/garden/office work in your area, and there are many people seeking work of this kind. Working in the actual kennels tends to be low-paid and although there may be many applicants for such jobs, finding suitable people to work with animals may not be quite so easy.

Maybe your predecessor employed staff who might wish to stay on and work for you. This can be very useful in the early days as you will have someone with local knowledge, and as long as there is an understanding that when you are the owner your methods must be followed, the takeover period may be considerably eased.

If you feel that you can manage very well but would find an extra pair of hands useful at the busiest times, namely weekends and holiday periods, contact the careers teacher at your local secondary school. There are many reliable youngsters who want to work with animals and need a weekend and holiday job. Sort out the applicants who still want to work in kennels once they understand all that it entails and you may find yourself a helper of considerable worth. Many a veterinary surgeon or veterinary nurse fostered the germ of a career with animals by working at the local boarding kennels during school holidays.

Accommodation

Daily workers or part-timers will need no accommodation other than decent washing and toilet facilities, plus of course somewhere to relax for a few minutes with a morning coffee or afternoon cup of tea; it is surprising how many kennels fail in this basic aspect of staff comfort though their licence insists they provide such facilities. If accommodation has to be provided for living-in staff, consider whether you would like to live in it before expecting anyone else to accept it. Many kennels provide caravan accommodation. Whether this is satisfactory depends on many things. While there are many people wanting to work in kennels a lot of them would not be able to tolerate sub-standard accommodation, which in any case they should not be offered. Kennels which provide excellent accommodation keep their staff. It is not fair to expect resident staff to live in squalor, and this can be seen at some kennels, knowing they would hate to leave their jobs because they really care for the boarders and their work. Without decent accommodation how can the staff have decent food? Without good, well balanced meals hard physical work is very hard indeed. A conscientious employer will think of the health and wellbeing of his staff as well as the health and comfort of the boarders.

Sometimes kennel maids' positions are advertised to 'live as family'. This is often a very satisfactory state of affairs with the employee's keep being deducted from the overall wage. However, care must be taken in selecting such staff as whoever lives in the house needs to be able to get along happily with all other members of the household. When this sort of situation works it is one of the best possible arrangements. There must be a happy 'family feeling' about the whole kennel whether staff live in or out, with consideration shown on both sides.

Staff training

Having chosen a new employee you will have to provide some training and have some rules, whether your helper is to work part- or full-time and regardless of whether he or she has worked in a kennel previously.

Security is the first subject you must impress upon your staff, in whatever capacity they work. They must always close gates and doors, and ensure that they are firmly latched to prevent escapes.

New recruits should be instructed in the correct methods of kennel cleaning and the basic daily routine. Learning to be an efficient kennel assistant is not achieved in one short, easy lesson: the daily routine of cleaning, exercising and feeding is only part of the job. It is equally important for kennel staff to be trained to be observant, to think for themselves, to watch and enjoy dogs and cats – however many years one works with animals, there will always be something different. Choose your kennel staff carefully and teach them well. Who knows, in time you may have a larger kennel and a school for kennel assistants!

Staff should be taught how to deal with clients in the best interests of all concerned. This means a friendly greeting whether in person or answering the telephone. It is more welcoming to answer the phone with, 'Beerode Kennels, may I help you?' than simply by saying 'Hello', or even 'Beerode 4321'. When meeting a client, they should address him or her by name, ask the pet's name – and remember it! Similarly, staff badges with a name on them – just 'Sally', 'Jimmy' or 'Jane' – is sufficient to help clients remember to whom they were talking. People often feel quite unsure about bringing their pets to a boarding kennel; if they find a friendly service their own confidence in your establishment is boosted.

Above all, remind your staff that no matter what toil, struggle or irritation any day may bring, kindness to the animals is paramount. The boarders' health, welfare, needs and comforts must always come first.

Some uniformity of clothing for kennel staff is smart and eye catching. There is nothing wrong with jeans, but patched, frayed or dirty jeans or slacks should not be tolerated. Even a simple tee shirt with the kennel name or logo overprinted would be attractive, or perhaps a tabard overall. Footwear needs to be clean and sturdy; wellington boots are the universal kennel footwear for much of the time but there is no need for them to look as though they have never been washed.

If you are interested in improving the professional image of the boarding kennel business you may wish to contact the Canine Studies Institute at Bracknell for details of the National Kennel Staff Training Certificate Course. The course provides some theoretical back-up for students who are receiving practical training at boarding and quarantine kennels.

Checking in

The kennel maid should be the one to take the new arrivals to their holiday accommodation, settle them into the kennel or cat chalet, make a little fuss of them – and return fairly soon to remind them they have not been forgotten. During the pet's visit it needs some tender loving care and kind words as well as an absolutely clean kennel and excellent food plus enjoyable exercise. The kennel staff should be able to attend to basic grooming during the stay.

Continuity of care is most important in the boarding kennel complex. The boarders are used to one person, mainly, caring for them at home and prefer to relate to one person; in your kennels the cat or dog will, albeit gradually, accept his or her kennel maid as 'Mum' for the duration. Continuity is therefore an important psychological aspect of care. It is also an important physical aspect, for the kennel maid who regularly attends to a group of animals may instinctively, or can be trained to, notice small irregularities which might be the forerunners of major problems.

Income tax and National Insurance

An employer is responsible for deducting income tax from his employees' pay, and non-collection can incur penalties. A free booklet, *Employer's Guide to PAYE*, is available from your local tax office, who will also supply you with deduction cards and code tables. The money deducted is paid to the tax office monthly, together with National Insurance contributions.

National Insurance deduction tables are provided by the Department of Social Security. The employer is responsible for deducting a weekly contribution from any employee earning more than £52 a week and he also *makes* a payment in respect of each employee.

Kennel work is one of the lower paid jobs and in many cases the kennel assistant's wage is below the statutory amount requiring the employer to pay National Insurance contributions. Low-paid staff should be aware that they may pay a voluntary NI contribution, but that it would be more beneficial to pay a self-employed category contribution, which is only a few pence higher, as this would entitle them to sickness benefits should the need arise. A visit to the local offices of the Ministry would provide you, and your staff, with all the relevant information.

Contract of employment

Each employee who works for 16 hours or more per week must receive a contract of employment (which can be in the form of a letter) setting out:

- Job title
- The rate of pay, and whether it is paid weekly or monthly
- Normal hours of work
- Holidays and holiday pay
- Provision for sick pay
- Pension and pension schemes
- Notice required by both parties
- Any disciplinary rules relating to the job
- Grievance procedures.

An itemised pay statement must be handed over with the pay giving:

- Gross wages
- Net wages
- Deductions and the reasons for them
- Details of any other payments.

Any employee who has worked for you continuously for 26 weeks or more must be given a written statement if you wish to dismiss him or her. One week's notice or payment in lieu is also due to the employee who has worked for over four weeks; after two years' continuous employment the employee is entitled to one week's notice for every year of continuous employment. If he or she feels unfairly treated, the employee can take the case to an industrial tribunal. You should familiarise yourself with leaflets on employment legislation issued by the Department of Employment, especially PL700: Written statement of main terms and conditions of employment, and PL699: Employment rights on the transfer of an undertaking.

Health hazards

Employers should ensure that kennel staff are inoculated against tetanus and that they receive boosters if necessary. Everyone who works in kennels should be covered by accident insurance, and employers should check that working conditions comply with the terms of the Health and Safety at Work Act 1974.

Certain people who work with animals may be considered as being at risk from rabies; employees at quarantine kennels could come into this category and in such cases vaccination against rabies is available to them. Such vaccinations are not available through the National Health Service and are quite expensive. Consult your doctor on this matter or the Vaccinating Centre, 53 Great Cumberland Place, London W1 7LH (0171-262 6456).

With the opening of the Eurotunnel in 1993 there is some concern that the danger of rabies occurring in Britain has been increased. Though we are assured that strict precautions are taken on both sides of the English Channel, the Eurotunnel presents an extra route for the greatest danger of all – the smuggling of pets into Britain.

It is essential that any suspicions of the illegal entry of dogs, cats or other small animals be reported to the authorities, and vigilance by knowledgeable people in the kennel business will be of vital importance. We must keep rabies out of Britain!

Chapter 10

Kennel Buildings

It is the kennel owners and their staff who make the boarding kennel popular and profitable, and the best kennel buildings in the world cannot compensate for inefficient management and an unpleasant manner. When you, as a prospective purchaser, visit a kennel which is being offered for sale, what makes the biggest impact on your mind is the first sight of the kennel property! What do you think your future clients will notice first? The outside runs and larger exercise areas or garden which meet the eye and are noted for their safety and attractive appearance, or their shabbiness, plethora of weeds and the reek of powerful disinfectant? Good disinfection need not involve strong or unpleasant odours. Safe, secure buildings need not resemble a prison.

Boarding kennel proprietors report that many people telephone to ask details of fees, but those who can be persuaded to visit a well situated and visually attractive kennel usually make firm bookings. Appearances obviously count for a great deal, though we know good management must run alongside.

Adapting existing property

If you see a property which you consider substandard, but which you feel you could improve easily, check first with the local authority to find out whether certain stipulated improvements have been recommended and whether or not you will be able to implement the council's requirements. It is possible that in some cases a district authority may allow improvements to be phased in gradually. Kennel owners who have been able to purchase what are apparently ideal kennels invariably find that there are still some improvements they wish to make.

Old pig sties or other farm buildings may have been converted into dog accommodation, sometimes with fairly satisfactory results. In other cases unfitted buildings have been converted into kennelling with the use of purpose-made galvanised mesh, solid galvanised sheet panels or partitioning. Various firms make galvanised kennel panelling, either mesh or solid, for indoor or outdoor use; set on levellers on good concrete flooring individual panels may be built up into any appropriate number of units, and in a suitable building are a very adequate form of kennelling.

Beware of the small cage accommodation too frequently offered to cats. Certain indoor catteries, as described in the Feline Advisory Bureau's own guide, are perfectly suitable for boarding, but any barn with a pile of cages described as a boarding cattery, or 'caravan used as cattery' as sometimes seen in advertisements should be viewed with suspicion. In such cramped accommodation the risk of infection is great enough to endanger the animals' health and thus be a threat to your business. Converted kennel accommodation usually depends on there being several securely fenced large outdoor exercise runs to which the boarders are taken individually several times a day as each kennel may not have the recommended adjoining run. Some boarding kennels advertise that all dogs are walked individually on leads every day, possibly because there is no securely fenced free outside exercise area. This can work well in a small kennel provided the owners are conscientious and can make time for it. Having to walk boarders on public roads because of lack of exercising areas within a kennel property is a security risk.

New designs

New designs in kennel buildings are coming into use and it is well worth visiting such places as the Wood Green Animal Shelters where circular buildings are proving highly satisfactory. For information contact Wood Green Animal Shelters, Heydon, Royston, Herts SG8 8PN, telephone 01763 838329.

The RSPCA kennels situated on the A22 near South Godstone in Surrey are also worth visiting by people who are thinking of starting boarding kennels. Telephone 01342 893117 for information.

A list of quarantine kennels may be obtained from the Ministry of Agriculture, Fisheries and Food (Animal Health Division), telephone 0181-330 4411. Visits to quarantine kennels are strictly by appointment only, but seeing several will show you that designs vary though all must work within MAFF regulations.

Conventional kennel accommodation

The recommended type of kennel accommodation will have attached runs. These designs fall into four main types:

1. an interior corridor with kennels on one side only, each
    kennel leading through to an individual run;
2. a central corridor with kennels on either side, each kennel
    leading to its individual run – the most satisfactory type
    generally, as the dogs can see friends across the aisle;
3. kennel compartments with a run attached, access being
    through the run to the kennel so that once the dog is shut
    in at night it might as well be shut in a large cupboard or coal
    bunker as it has no contact with, or view of, any other dog;
4. purpose-built kennel units with a central corridor, but instead
    of bars or mesh there are solid doors and partitions on each
    side of the corridor – although this plan may reduce noise, as
    the dogs cannot see into the central corridor, neither can the
    kennel staff see the dogs.

Generally speaking, the second type of corridor kennels is the
easiest to manage, and the most appreciated by the pets. Many
have the access hatch to the run area opened both from outside the
run gate and from inside the corridor. Cleaning of inside kennels
when the dogs are in the runs is easy, and when the inside cleaning
and disinfecting is over it is a simple matter to attend to the outside
runs.

Outside runs attached to kennels are most satisfactory if they
are separated from each other by 3-feet high solid walls topped
with galvanised mesh panels to give a 6-feet high division. Such
compartments are the easiest to keep clean. Runs may be partially
covered to provide shelter, or fully mesh covered to deter the
fence-climbing escape artists. When choosing mesh gates always
check the fastenings for firm closing. Clever dogs can work out
ways of opening anything which is not absolutely paw proof.

In addition to security within the kennel buildings the boarding
kennel owner must also secure the property against intruders. This
means secure perimeter fencing and locked gates after business
hours. It also means that your property should not be left
unattended. Dogs and puppies have been stolen from boarding
kennels so, when thinking of security, remember it is a two-way
problem.

The kennel corridors themselves are important. A corridor
which is too narrow can be difficult when manipulating cleaning
equipment or when two people are working in the same kennel
and passing each other in the corridor. Four feet is a comfortable
width for easy working and cleaning. Some corridors have gullies
(with or without gratings) to carry away excess cleaning water

PURPOSE BUILT KENNEL BLOCK

KENNEL BUILDING INTERIOR

A – WINDOW
B – INFRA-RED HEATER OVER BED
C – DOOR
D – DRAFT EXCLUDER
E – FOOD & WATER BOWLS
F – PULL-UP DOOR TO RUN
G – PULLEY TO OPERATE OUTER DOOR
H – EXPELAIR HEATER-BLOWER
J – SINK
K – SECURITY DOOR
L – WATER HEATER
M – SHELVING
N – SLIDING DOORS
P – MAIN ENTRANCE

KENNELS AND PART-COVERED RUNS

GATE

SAFETY CORRIDOR

GATE

CONCRETED RUNS
WITH COVERED AREA

INDOOR KENNEL

DOOR TO RUN

INTERIOR CENTRAL CORRIDOR

WELD MESH

COVERED ROOF

PENTHOUSE CATTERY

SECURITY FENCING

CONCRETE

and often these are not deep enough to deal with the flow so floods occur. Some purpose-designed manufactured units cater for a corridor only 2 ft 6 in wide. One water point, or more in a really long building, is a necessity. A permanently attached hose is also useful in case of fire.

In addition to the runs attached to kennels, it is advantageous to have other larger and securely fenced runs where the dogs can play twice a day. Grass or pebble surfaced runs need to be paved around the perimeter and at the entrance, both for tidiness and to deter escapees from tunnelling under the wire.

In wooden kennels, cat chalets or penthouses, there should be an inner lining which is treated with an impermeable, washable paint. Non-lead paints, of course, and no creosote for kennel or cattery woodwork. Creosote is toxic and takes ages to dry; it stains everything. Cuprinol is not harmful to dogs or cats, though the cedar colour may rub off a little on to light-coloured coats.

Chain link fencing, which is usually used for the larger exercise runs, needs to be sunk in concrete below the ground surface, and the intervals between the supporting irons or posts should not be too great. Chain link fencing is regularly advertised in the weekly dog papers by such firms as Jacksons whose brochures describe both galvanised and green PVC-coated chain link fencing, posts and gates. Outside perimeter fencing of chain link needs to have jump-deterring jackal type fencing, ie taut wire strands sloping inwards atop 6 feet high chain link.

Boarding establishments which do not have attached covered runs to each individual kennel would find it extremely useful to have at least one outside covered exercise area, securely fenced, for use when the weather is doing its worst. Grass on outside runs needs periodic resting, and pebble surfaces can be changed occasionally. Pebble runs dry quickly after rain; many dogs enjoy and prefer grass as that is the normal surface for them at home, but keep the grass short or small dogs with long coats will get soaked after heavy dew or rain.

Isolation units
All kennels and catteries are required by law to have an isolation unit. This does not have to be extensive but separate units situated away from other boarders should be provided for dogs and cats and there should be accommodation for a few sick animals.

Walls
Kennel walls need to have an impermeable, easy to clean, surface. Breeze block walls need painting with a non-lead paint; an industrial one-coat cover-all emulsion is good as the job has to be repeated frequently since regular wall washing and disinfecting, as well as scratching and chewing, takes a heavy toll of the decor. Breeze blocks with a smooth, impervious tile face remove the need for painting, as does the use of semi-engineering brick. Always keep your eyes open for materials which will lessen your maintenance problems. The important points to remember when choosing a design or kennel plan are to be sure that (a) the building layout and materials are suitable under the Animal Boarding Establishments Act 1963, (b) they are easy to care for and (c) the boarders can be happy and comfortable in them.

Certain accident precautions should be borne in mind. For example, small mesh wire should be used for cat unit runs as chain link would allow a cat's head to slip through and possibly become wedged. If the chain link mesh used for kennel runs is too large, small dogs may try to get through and become stuck, sometimes with disastrous consequences. The purpose-made galvanised mesh panels used for kennel runs have many safety features.

Floors

Kennel floors need to be impermeable to water and other liquids. This usually means concrete, though kennels for smaller dogs may be tiled – either with quarry tiles or, where damage by the occupants is likely to be negligible, with vinyl tiles. Toy dog breeds and cats are usually less hard on their surroundings, and some district authorities still approve wooden-floored buildings. Generally speaking, wooden kennel buildings are not recommended, except for cats, but this policy is one to discuss with the local authority as opinions vary.

Concrete floors need to be treated with a sealant or dust retardant. Raw concrete is not only dusty but is very porous and can harbour round worm eggs. As urine and disinfectants can also penetrate porous concrete, it can become very smelly and unhygienic. Details of concrete sealers can be obtained from companies such as Compotect and Watco (Sales) Ltd. There are products for use on concrete outdoors and indoors, and it is important to use the right product in the right place. Concrete treatments are, unfortunately, not inexpensive and you should consult the industrial flooring experts for their advice, as the products themselves are not as easy to use as a tin of emulsion paint; in fact they can be very difficult, and professional application is advised.

Kitchens

The ideal is for each kennel building to have its own food storage, preparation and serving area, plus storage space for dishes and cleaning equipment. The food preparation area should be equipped with a hot water supply as well as cold – for washing dishes, obviously, and because disinfectants used in buckets of hot water are more efficient. There should also be at least a simple cooking arrangement, even if it is only a hotplate. As the ideal in this case is not very easy to find, consider whether you can make better arrangements than those shown to you when you are looking at kennels with a view to purchasing.

Gates

Kennel gates may vary from solid (in which case we are back to that 'shutting in the cupboard' position) to mesh or bars. One of the best kennel gate plans is manufactured by Athag whose barred gates have a special device whereby water bowls are held in place (less spillage) and food bowls can be put into kennels without entering the kennel itself, both a time-saving device and very useful with difficult dogs. It is also a safety precaution to foil the quick escape artist! Athag also manufacture solid partitions in a see-through material; this is particularly useful when an impermeable barrier is required, as it is always desirable to see into a kennel and much more fun for the dogs if they can see out. Quarantine kennels and indoor catteries would find such equipment worth considering.

Radio

An extremely useful small appliance in the boarding kennel is the radio. Relatively inexpensive, probably filched from the household, it provides a touch of home from home and the sound of human voices, or music, for the dogs. It helps to keep some dogs quiet by distracting them from outside noises which might otherwise be the signal for a really good barking session.

Heating

Some boarding kennels and quarantine kennels charge extra for heating. It would be safer to include it in the basic fees or a boarder's owner might well say the pet does not require heating when it really should have it, regardless of the fact that all your kennels are heated anyway.

Some kennels prefer to use only part of their complex during the winter, as bookings will be fewer and it is more economical to have part of the premises comfortably heated and well booked than to have some buildings with only one or two occupants needing warmth. Draught exclusion and insulation help to reduce heating costs.

Heating used in kennels must be safe and fume-free. Paraffin heaters and calor gas stoves have too many potential dangers to leave unattended in any building, let alone in one used for animal housing. Central heating from an oil or gas fired boiler would prove ideal, but whether it is feasible to install such a heating unit depends on many things.

Electric, fan-assisted, warm air heating, thermostatically controlled, is ideal, such as an Expelair. Some properties may be blessed with 'off peak' or 'white meter' electricity charges which are a great advantage. However, the Economy 7 plan may not be suited to kennel use as the connected appliances do not start taking in heat until about 1 am, and when they are giving off good heat it is time to open up the kennels and let out the dogs – and the heat too. Also, it can be extremely cold between 4 pm and 1 am in the depths of winter. Some other form of back-up heating would be necessary, so the system would not prove as economical in this context as it may in a purely domestic situation.

One of the most useful forms of kennel heating, for both dogs and cats, is the infra-red dull emitter lamp suspended over the sleeping area of the kennel or cat unit. The Wren Foster Ray dull emitter available from Diamond Edge is one of the best known of its kind and consists of a 'bulb' which gives warmth but no light, and looks rather like a small terra cotta plant pot. It is available in various wattages and can be hung high or low in a kennel, out of reach of the dog. Heaters can be thermostatically controlled or fitted with a dimmer switch. Naturally, only the kennels which are occupied need to have the heater on. The clear red glass lamps which give both light and heat are more prone to breakage, or they may keep the dogs awake at night with resultant midnight barking, but at least you have a choice.

Other forms of electric heating used in kennels and catteries are the tubular greenhouse heaters, again attached to a thermostatic control. There are also electrically heated strong plastic beds available, and some heated pads for use in non-heated beds, though the latter devices are more suited to breeding kennels than to boarding kennels. Despite claims that the electrical connections are safe, one wonders if the makers have ever seen just how much damage a determined dog can do once it starts.

Chapter 11

Fanfare

Come blow your horn! You have purchased your boarding kennel, moved in and must advertise your presence. Advertising can cost a lot of money or relatively little, depending on who you are trying to attract to your business and how you set about the task.

Trade sign

If yours is a domestic boarding business, as opposed to a quarantine kennel, it is most likely that the majority of your clients will come from your immediate area or within a radius of 10 to 15 miles. This is the area to saturate with regular advertising; the people need to know about you and the service you offer. To begin with, the 'Under New Management' tag attracts attention and if your kennel has a sign at the entrance, add it to this. 'Under new management' shows that you are neither sheltering behind your predecessor's goodwill nor are afraid to take up the challenge of building your own reputation. It may be necessary to consult the local authority planning department before a trade sign is erected, particularly if your property is down a country lane and you would like a directional sign on land which you do not own.

Have you ever considered a kennel logo, your very own trade mark? If there is someone in your family with artistic talent, make use of this and perhaps your own kennel logo will emerge and become an eye-catching symbol on your stationery and advertisements, on your car or van. Pictures are remembered, and the simpler they are the quicker they catch the eye.

Advertising

Which local paper do most people in your catchment area read? The answer is, most probably, 'The paper which is delivered free!' Such papers are supported solely by advertising and your advertisement would be worth the investment in the classified column which caters for pets. You may also wish to try other local papers; when you receive enquiries check which paper brings the best results.

Your advertisements will of necessity be brief, but they should indicate whether you board dogs and cats, or only one species, whether you give any additional service such as grooming, whether you specialise in large breeds – sufficient information to attract the attention and bring enquiries. A displayed advertisement in the local paper is usually the most advantageous, and your first might read something like the following:

BEERODE BOARDING KENNELS
(Under New Management)
SUPERIOR ACCOMMODATION
for
DOGS and CATS
Phone Beerode 4321

Smart advertising reaps rewards and not all of it need be in the form of paid insertions in newspapers. The aim should be to keep your business name in the public eye in as many ways as possible.

The Yellow Pages list dog and cat boarding establishments under 'Boarding Kennels'. If you bought an existing business, the telephone number should have been part of the deal, and still be in the directories. If you are starting up, get your name included in the Yellow Pages as well as the ordinary directory; the extra cost for a display advertisement will be a few hundred pounds. Find out if there are any other trade directories for your area. Is there a town guide?

Although the majority of your clients will come from the local catchment area, many people are willing to travel considerable distances to board their pets in a kennel, particularly a cattery, which is recommended or which they have used previously and found satisfactory. Plan advertising to cover this wider area.

A small advertisement occasionally in the specialist kennel magazine, *Kennel and Cattery Management*, or *Our Dogs*, *Dog World* or *Cats* will make your name known nationwide. Emphasise any specialised facilities you may have, such as reductions for several dogs from one kennel while the owner takes a holiday; whether you can take over someone's breeding kennel, should the owner unfortunately become ill; whether your kennels are particularly suited to large breeds; whether you can offer specialist care for Tibetan breeds, Poodles, guard dogs, or whatever is your particular interest. Boarding needs are not confined only to the local pets whose owners are taking their annual vacation.

A further, and very important, medium for advertising your kennel is in publications and at locations concerned entirely with the armed forces. Many forces families are pet owners and the very nature of a forces career entails comings and goings and, therefore, the boarding of pets. If your kennel is situated anywhere near a service base, contact the relevant officer and ask about means of advertising your presence to forces families. Visit the local NAAFI store and note which forces magazines and newspapers are on sale and enquire the advertising rates from the publishers.

Beware of advertising your kennels as an animal sanctuary as this may imply that your business is a charity, which it is not. Avoid advertising that you take in rescued dogs. Yes, your kennel may well offer sanctuary to some pets on occasions, but you are running a business and official animal sanctuaries usually seek registered charity status.

Unfortunately, you may find that some people will consider your kennels as a sanctuary anyway; to put it more bluntly, some will look on your premises as a dumping ground for animals they no longer wish to keep. Word your advertisements to discourage this behaviour. This serious matter is also referred to in Chapter 5.

If your advertising campaign works well and the bookings mount up you will find that there are times when you are very busy indeed, and nice though this thought may be, be careful not to overbook. So often, everyone wants to bring the pet along on a Friday, but nobody wants to collect until Saturday, or even Monday. For this reason some kennels keep a 'change-over' kennel – a building which is not booked except to accommodate an overflow at such times. However, many boarding kennel owners would be quite happy if their only problems were concerned with accommodating an overflow of boarders!

Telephone enquiries

As enquiries will mostly be made by phone, it follows that whoever answers must sound welcoming and be fully informed of boarding fees and services. The information must be kept in the office handy to the telephone.

You have to be your own salesman and 'sell' your kennel to the client. Ask for some special information about the caller's dog or cat, say something nice about the breed, or dogs and cats in general if the pet cannot claim to belong to any particular breed, build a little confidence, invite the caller to visit your kennels, by appointment of course. It is impossible to quote for grooming services to new clients until you have seen the dog: another reason to suggest a visit. Many owners think their pets have well kept coats but when the canine beautician starts to work on it, the amount of time needed to rescue the dog from its matted mantle may far outweigh the original estimate in time and money. Regular clients in the grooming department, if you have one, are a different matter altogether.

Stationery

You will probably be ordering new kennel stationery and handouts for prospective clients and need to consider what information you should include. Use the kennel logo and think whether it is best to say a lot or a little.

Your kennel stationery should include booking forms and brochures. These can be designed to suit your own needs and to tell your own story. Prospective clients will need a booking application form, either given to them when they visit the kennel or sent by post to enquirers. The booking form should be designed to establish all the information you need to know about the boarders and the owners, and contain some basic things they need to know about your kennels. It becomes a contract between you and the client and both parties are expected to honour the contract. As booking forms need to be filed in your office while the boarders are in residence with you, they have to be reasonably substantial, and they must be in duplicate so that both you and the pet owner have a copy. A sample booking application form is shown on page 50.

The brochure, which tells more about how you care for the dogs, is a handout you may want to use for general advertising purposes as well as for sending to clients with the booking form. Considerable care needs to be taken in preparing the brochure which lists your conditions of boarding.

Your exact location, with a small map if necessary, should be shown and your opening times should be clearly stated. It should list your boarding fees and any circumstances under which they may be altered. Any extras which the fees include – heating and insurance for example – should be mentioned. Your brochure should make it clear how your fees are applied; for example, if a dog arrives on Monday afternoon and departs the following Monday morning will you charge seven or eight days' fees? It should also be stated that fees are payable in advance or at the time of departure, that cheques will not be accepted without a banker's card and that no booking is guaranteed unless a deposit, non-returnable, is paid in advance. Make it known whether you are closed on bank holidays, and whether you are closed on one day during the week or have a half-day closing.

Make it quite clear that no animals are accepted to board unless they have a current certificate of vaccination against the most prevalent diseases and that absolutely no exception can be made for not presenting an up-to-date immunisation certificate. The health of your boarders and the reputation of your kennel depend on it.

Owners may be reminded that their pets are usually happier if they have their own beds and bedding (though you will have supplies for them if required) – it reminds the dogs of home. It is a good idea to encourage owners to bring their dog's towel, very useful in wet weather because the dogs will have to be dried after exercise. Mention whether you have a grooming service and make it clear whether it is a trimming and grooming service for all breeds or a simple brush and tidy up before the dogs go home. A full trimming service involves an extra charge, but a routine brush and combing should be inclusive.

State that you feed the dogs a well balanced diet and use the best quality food; make sure that you do! Let people know that the boarders' usual food will be taken into consideration. You could allow any owner to bring special supplies for the pet.

Local activities

What else can you do? Become known in the local dog and cat show community even though you may not be an exhibitor and do not wish to become involved in either dog or cat breeding. Local breeders and exhibitors are often approached for recommendations to boarding kennels; they cannot recommend yours if they do not know anything about it or you. Contact your local canine society or cat club; the names of the secretaries can be obtained from the Kennel Club or the Governing Council of the Cat Fancy if you do not already know them. Find out if there is a ringcraft or obedience training class in your area. Go along to it, and take some brochures with you. These local societies will probably have a series of competitive events during the course of the year. Most of them are struggling along on a shoestring – you know the feeling! Offer a special prize or rosettes; a small investment, but your kennel name will appear on the literature: 'Best-in-Match Rosette presented by Beerode Kennels' – good advertising among people in a position to pass on your name to others. Take time out to go to the weekly ringcraft or obedience class, volunteer your services as a steward, offer to make the tea, just make yourself useful – and *known* in the local small animal community.

Local canine societies usually produce a newsletter – if they don't, suggest they start one, and lend a helping hand. Newsletters are great places for very inexpensive advertising, as are the societies' show schedules and catalogues. Of course, you will be very busy in the summer months but shows and match meetings are held all the year round. They are friendly, enjoyable activities; helpers are always needed. In return for your help, or a donation towards rosettes, your name appears in the club literature.

In addition to mingling with the local professional dog and cat breeders and exhibitors, find out what general business organisations there are in your locality. You are the proprietor of a legitimate business and can meet other businessmen on equal terms. Besides, some of them are probably dog owners. You will be patronising their establishments; they in turn may patronise yours. Cultivate the other owner-operated businesses; the giant multiples are very impersonal. You can do a week's shopping in a hypermarket and never speak a word to anyone. Visit small traders and exchange the time of day; introduce yourself; be your own ambassador and sales executive. Traders often display small advertisement cards for a minimum charge: make use of these facilities.

Keep an eye on the local paper for news of what is going on at meetings of the parish and district councils. Are they making new by-laws about dogs? What about licensing? Are they complaining about dogs being a nuisance? Find out who is your representative and make sure you put him or her right on these doggy matters. Who is your Member of Parliament? Find out his or her views on new laws being considered concerning dog control and licensing; make your own reasoned views known. Your business may be at stake. Take an active part in community affairs. Yes, it will be hard to find the time, but if you do not stand up you may not be recognised.

Another good advertisement comes free of charge – free of extra charge anyway. You will need an estate car or a small van: see that it carries the name of your kennel, your logo if any, and your telephone number. Wherever you go around your neighbourhood the van can do your advertising for you. Park it in a prominent place; be sure the lettering is clear and easy to read and that the vehicle is always sparkling clean, as it reflects the image of your business.

Ask your local veterinary practice if your kennel name and address can be displayed on the notice board in their reception area. In fact, if you put your mind to it you may be able to think of several extra ways of keeping your kennel name in the public eye so that it will be remembered when somebody needs boarding accommodation for their pets.

Let it be known that visitors to your kennels are welcome, but insist on an appointment and make it quite clear that visitors, who may be future clients, do not touch any of the boarders. Not only may the visitors be carrying a few germs but the boarders may not want to be touched, and the visitors will be impressed with your care – whether for their safety or the dogs' matters not in this instance. Hopefully they will remember you when their pets, or their friends' pets, need boarding accommodation. With cats, the 'do not touch' regulation is mandatory. Only the cattery attendant or the owners touch the cats; they are much more easily subject to infections, and many can be lightning quick with a disapproving paw!

Unlicensed competition

Having considered all possible ways of advertising your kennels, bear in mind that your very best advertisements are happy, well cared for dogs and cats, and satisfied owners. Remember, too, that other licensed boarding kennels in your area have every right to advertise their services but keep a wary eye open for certain forms of unlicensed competition which are a threat to you and other licensed kennel operators too. There are people who advertise in the local paper or on postcards in shop windows, 'Your pets cared for in my home during your holidays', or some similar wording.

There is another form of direct competition from certain organisations or individuals who advertise that they will 'dog sit' in private homes while the owners are away, or will visit the property regularly to walk the dogs and feed them. Charges levied for these sitters' services are often higher than your professional fees would be and, of course, other people are using the owners' home facilities and there is no guarantee against burglary, despite advertised claims. There is, of course, no reason why a person should not look after a dog for a friend; however, if such services are advertised under the heading of 'boarding accommodation' or in any way imply that dog or cat boarding facilities are being offered, the licensed boarding kennel owner who uses the same advertising medium has good reason to complain to the publisher, as the legitimately licensed business has to fulfil certain stringent conditions of security and care and is paying for long-term advertising in the paper. You can make known to potential clients that dogs and cats are disturbed by their owners' absence. The pet left at an insecurely fenced private house may decide to leave and search for its own home. Pets suddenly finding different people inhabiting the home in its owner's place may be equally disturbed and act accordingly, possibly even resenting and becoming aggressive towards the strangers.

Private home boarding may undercut your prices. Place a postcard ad of your own emphasising professional, approved and licensed kennels where pets are secure and cared for by trained staff.

Chapter 12

Expanding Your Business

How to make the business more profitable is always in the mind of the boarding kennel owner who is trying to become established. Although it may be little comfort when things are slow, it is a proven fact that any business to do with small animal care grows on personal recommendation of satisfied clients. The bulk of your bookings will come in the recognised holiday months as so many pet-owning families have children, and school holidays dictate family vacation dates. Therefore, much of the repeat business is on an annual basis.

Increased capacity

Perhaps the first thing to consider is that as some kennels have become established, they have found a need for more kennel accommodation. If you are considering adding some more dog kennels why not research the sort of accommodation generally offered in your area? Are the really large breeds well catered for? Does anybody specialise in the toy breeds? Is there a kennel offering super luxury accommodation to the truly pampered pet? It is quite surprising that although most of the population want to find the cheapest boarding accommodation for their pets, there is a firm following for the luxury kennelling which is advertised infrequently. Infrequently? Is that a clue in itself? Perhaps your area could do with some five-star accommodation for discerning pets? All mod cons and personal radio.

Think very hard before you add a cattery to an existing dog boarding kennel. It is not ideal for the feline species to be boarded in close association with their canine brethren, but many owners might look on it as the ideal expansion of the business because they believe a cattery means less work and more money. Do not believe that! It depends a great deal on the area in which your business is situated.

Before considering the addition of a cattery, find out how many other catteries there are in your area, how many are separate organisations and how many are run in conjunction with dog boarding establishments. Only too frequently a cat owner's attitude is to leave the cat in the care of a neighbour at holiday time and not bother with formal boarding; a wrong attitude of course, but one which has an effect on your business.

Grooming services

There is considerable interest at present in dog grooming and trimming – the work of the canine beautician. This is an all-year-round business except for a slack spell in January or February, though the first spring sunshine brings the clients back for trimming.

Before you think of starting a grooming service in conjunction with your kennels, consider whether you are trained for that particular job, or whether any member of your staff is an experienced canine beautician. Canine beauticians must be trained and it is not a job which can be learned from scratch on a very short course. Training can be very expensive, both from the point of view of tuition for the beginner and the cost of the equipment. It is also necessary to have a proper grooming room – which may perhaps double as a dispensary – a large bath with a shower spray and hot and cold water, of course. A large, very steady table is needed, and a good light. Perhaps, most of all, it is important to realise that bathing, blow drying, trimming and styling a dog takes time, and it is not a job which should have too many interruptions.

If you wish to offer a grooming service to existing clients it would probably be considered an ancillary part of your kennel business and would not require 'change of use' permission. If you have not trimmed dogs before you may wish to get in touch with the Professional Groomers Association which is part of the Pet Trade and Industry Association (address page 142).

Should you not wish to take a training course yourself but would like to offer a trimming service, there may be a local canine beautician who would be prepared to work at your kennels on some arranged basis, or you may wish to employ a kennel maid who is also a trained beautician. Either of these suggestions presupposes that you have a suitable grooming room and bathing facilities. Most trained trimmers own their equipment.

As dogs such as Poodles and American Cocker Spaniels need trimming and bathing every six to eight weeks, and luxury coated breeds need a professional grooming at about the same interval of time, and as Terriers and other Spaniel breeds need stripping two or three times a year, you could have an interesting, and paying, ancillary business to your boarding kennel, and also a continuity of contact with your clients.

Although canine beauty equipment is quite expensive to buy, it lasts for years with regular care and servicing. Naturally, some grooming jobs are particularly hard on the equipment, *and* the groomer, for many people allow their Old English Sheepdogs or Afghans to become matted solid and such work is heavy and tiring. With perseverance you can encourage these wayward owners to become regular clients and thus make life a lot better for the dogs, which are often very uncomfortable when their coats are full of mats and tangles.

Product sales

People who board their dogs with you are a pet product purchasing population. A kennel owner is in a good position to advise on suitable types of collars and leads, feeding bowls, pet toys and pet foods, and sell them. Again, if these services are offered as an ancillary to your business, no official objections should be raised. However, if you wish to establish a fully fledged retail shop, consult the district authority first. Many councils restrict retail outlets to certain commercial areas.

A number of kennels sell foodstuffs to their clients, another continuing trade. Ask yourself if your kennel is situated in a good position for this to be a viable proposition, remembering the pet owner's tendency to buy the pet food along with the weekly groceries at the supermarket. So much depends on whether you have a good trading position and permission to open a 'Canine Cash and Carry'.

Should you decide not to become involved with ancillary trades at your kennel, you might look for other ways of keeping the kennels occupied. Sometimes boarding kennels are asked to accept police dogs – that is, their own dogs, not strays. If you have suitable kennels for large dogs this may be a possibility. The police sometimes have dogs arriving for assessment and need extra accommodation for them. Contact your county constabulary on this matter.

Occasionally accommodation is required for guard dogs, and by charitable organisations for rescue dogs. Whether or not you will want to become involved with strays or rescue dogs (as they are likely not to have been inoculated) is questionable; you would be defeating your most important health rule in accepting such dogs.

Sometimes other kennel owners, either boarding kennel folk or the owners of breeding/exhibiting kennels, need to take a break. If you are prepared to offer a service to these people an advertisement in the weekly dog press would be noticed, or if you are interested in a particular breed, try to keep a small running ad going in the breed club magazine. These latter advertisements are usually quite inexpensive and bring results.

Puppy rearing

Many boarding kennel owners come into the business via the show dog world and may find they have extra income from puppy sales. However, much depends on the breed which is their particular interest and whether there is a demand for puppies. If you have more than two breeding bitches you may find that you will have to apply for a breeder's licence under the Breeding of Dogs Act 1973. Puppy rearing, if done properly, is a very time-consuming occupation, and is also very expensive. Profits are made only by cutting costs in every possible way, to the probable detriment of the puppies themselves, and by selling them at six weeks when many of them are not ready to go to new homes. There is also the problem of disease, and many intensive puppy breeding units were wiped out by canine parvovirus disease in the late 1970s and early 80s. Although there are now vaccines against this disease, baby pups are particularly vulnerable.

It is known that some boarding kennels have in the past bought in puppies from puppy farmers for resale locally. Resist this temptation with all your might! Buying in puppies in bulk is a heartless trade and leads to nothing but grief and woe.

There is one service you might like to consider offering in your area . . . a special service to senior citizens. It is quite likely that older people would appreciate a break from the responsibility of their animal companions occasionally, perhaps while they visit relatives or maybe because they have to spend a few days in hospital. You could advertise special concessions for senior citizen pet owners at certain times. It would be better to offer such a service regularly, perhaps one week a month outside the peak periods, in order to keep a continuity of trade, contracts and recommendations flowing all the time. You may also be doing some pets a service too, as often their elderly owners forget to groom them, or maybe are unable to groom them or exercise the pets sufficiently.

Quarantine kennels

It should be clearly understood that quarantine kennels are not for people who have had no previous experience of dogs, although this aspect of kennel ownership may appear attractive and lucrative, and is an all year round trade. Considerable experience, preferably of domestic boarding kennel management, is necessary though occasionally a quarantine establishment may be the first, and very successful, purchase for the owners. In such cases, the new owners may be taking on experienced staff, and may also have years of business experience in management and executive positions.

Nevertheless, quarantine is a branch of the kennel business to which many aspire, and if you have a boarding kennel which seems suitable for expansion in this way, what points should you consider? Dogs and cats, and certain other animals, which are brought into any part of the United Kingdom and Eire, must be imported under licence and serve six months' quarantine detention at a quarantine kennel approved by the Ministry of Agriculture, Fisheries and Food in the UK or by the Department of Agriculture in Eire. Certain other countries, of which Australia and New Zealand are the best known, will not import dogs and cats unless the animals have served their six months' quarantine in a rabies-free country such as ours, or unless they were born here or have lived here for a specified period of time. Therefore, there are many dogs and cats in our quarantine kennels which are in transit from another country to Australia or New Zealand. Once the six months' detention has been served the dogs and cats remain on British soil in a non-quarantine environment – perhaps in the domestic section of the quarantine kennel – for a further specified time awaiting shipment to their future destinations. Obviously, quarantine kennels have a certain continuity of business which ordinary domestic boarding lacks.

Experienced owners of an existing domestic boarding business should consider carefully the suitability of their property and its location for quarantine purposes and should then contact their Divisional Veterinary Officer or one of the addresses given on pages 136–137. Enquirers will receive full details concerning all aspects of operating a quarantine kennel, which will be subject to the control of the Ministry. The Ministry has detailed provisions for the design, construction, operation and management of authorised quarantine premises.

Planning permission will be needed from the local authority and an application must be made to the Ministry of Agriculture, Fisheries and Food: no work on a proposed kennel should be undertaken until approval has been obtained in writing from both. A further requirement is that the owner shall nominate a Veterinary Superintendent who will undertake overall control of the premises, as the latter will be responsible to the Ministry for all aspects of the establishment. Quarantine establishments receive regular inspections on behalf of the Ministry and, of course, all requirements must be met or the licence may be jeopardised. Owners of quarantine kennels will be required to cooperate with any alterations in the regulations which may be deemed necessary by the Ministry according to changing circumstances; continuation of the licence will depend on the owner's ability to comply with changed regulations.

All the problems associated with dogs and cats coming into domestic boarding kennels are magnified considerably in quarantined animals which have probably made a long, and not altogether comfortable, air journey of many thousands of miles in a secure crate and then been driven to your kennel before being released . . . still to be deprived of a sniff at British grass for another six months! Stress on the animal is multiplied to an enormous degree, and the care which must be provided by the quarantine kennel staff is increased.

Show dogs are imported quite regularly and people who have worked overseas particularly members of the armed forces, bring their pets home with them. In fact, one of the best ways of advertising quarantine accommodation is in the military magazines and newspapers. Of course, alongside quarantine business is shipping – importing and exporting – and naturally the 'Q' kennel needs to be a licensed carrier for quarantine-bound dogs and cats.

There have been some recent changes to our quarantine regulations, and there have also been suggestions that as rabies vaccines have been improved in recent years, quarantine regulations may be altered further, or perhaps eventually abandoned altogether. So far the only alteration has been to allow 'traded dogs' to come to Britain, provided that they come from a registered kennel in one of the EU countries, were born in that kennel and vaccinated against rabies at the age of three months, were tested for rabies immunity at six months, and have not been outside their European registered kennel during those six months. They must also have been implanted with a microchip giving their identity and vaccination status, and travel to a registered kennel in Britain. On arrival here, such dogs are again tested for immunity to rabies and, if immune, are then free to travel anywhere in the UK. As far as is known, dogs imported under this regulation so far have all been potential show dogs destined for exhibition and breeding purposes in Britain, and would have come into quarantine for the statutory six months prior to the relaxation of that regulation. Other dogs and cats being brought to Britain from any country are, at present, still subject to the statutory six months quarantine requirement.

Whether the above relaxation of the quarantine regulations which have served our country so well, and which have been of assistance to other countries too, will be further relaxed in view of improved vaccines and some public opinion which labels quarantine as 'cruel', remains to be seen. In these circumstances it would be wise for any boarding kennel owners who are considering adding quarantine accommodation to their present kennels, or people purchasing a boarding kennel which already has quarantine accommodation, to contact their Divisional Veterinary Officer or the office of the Ministry of Agriculture, Fisheries and Food for their area for the latest information, as changes in quarantine regulations obviously affect the boarding kennel business.

Enquiries concerning quarantine kennels should be addressed to your Divisional Veterinary Officer, whose address may be obtained from your own veterinary surgeon, or to the address overleaf which is most appropriate to your area:

Ministry of Agriculture, Fisheries and Food
Animal Health Division, Hook Rise South,
Tolworth, Surbiton, Surrey KT6 7NF; 0181–330 4411

Department of Agriculture and Fisheries for Scotland
Animal Health Division, Pentland House,
47 Robbs Loan, Edinburgh EH14 1SQ; 0131–556 8400

Welsh Office Agriculture Department
Crown Buildings, cathays Park,
Cardiff CF1 3NQ; 0267 234545

Ministry of Agriculture, Fisheries and Food for Northern Ireland
Dundonald House, Upper Newtownards Road,
Belfast BT4 3SB; 01232 650111

Department of Agriculture
Agriculture House, Dublin 2, Eire; 010 353 1 789011

Appendix

Useful addresses

Grooming Equipment

Allbrooks Ltd, 9 Curzon Road, Chilton Industrial Estate, Sudbury, Suffolk CO10 6XW

Diamond Edge Ltd, 126 Gloucester Road, Brighton BN1 4BU; 01273 605922

Petcetera Etc Ltd, PO Box 112, Henley-in-Arden, Solihull, West Midlands B95 5HD; 01614 803373

Shaws Pet Products Ltd, 50 Weston Road, Aston Clinton, Aylesbury, Buckinghamshire HP22 5EH; 01296 630121

Heating and Infra-red lamps
Diamond Edge Ltd, Address above

Insurance
Dog Breeders Insurance Co Ltd, Freepost, Bournemouth BH2 6BR; 01202 295771

Pet Plan Group Ltd, Westcross House, 2 Westcross Way, Brentford, Middlesex TW8 9DX; 0181–580 8000

Kennel buildings and equipment
Athag (Guardsman) Ltd, Carlyon Road, Industrial Estate, Atherstone, Warwickshire CV9 1LQ; 01827 713768

M A Drayton Ltd, 16 Morton Road, Laughton, Gainsborough, Lincolnshire DN21 3PS; 01427 628381

Jacksons Fencing, 6 Stowting Common, Nr Ashford, Kent TN25 6BN; 01233 750393

KonKrete Manufacturing Co, Woodend Works, Redbrook Street, Woodchurch, Ashford, Kent TN26 3QU; 01233 860561

A Neaverson & Sons Ltd, Peakirk, Nr Peterborough PE6 7NN; 01733 252225

D Scott (Buildings) Ltd, Bridge Street, Thrapston, Northamptonshire NN14 4LR; 01832 732366

Kennel property

The Kennels Agency, 11 Church Street, Twyford, Reading, Berkshire RG10 9DR; 01734 345676

Kennel Sales, 'The Gordons', 73 The Green, Ewell, Epsom, Surrey KT17 3JX; 0181–394 0833

Kennel supplies and maintenance

Compotect, Compotect House, Kelvin Road, Elland, West Yorkshire HX5 0LL; 01422 376804

Lever Brothers Ltd, (Domestos), Lever House, 3 St James Road, Kingston-upon-Thames, Surrey KT1 2BA; 0181 541 8200

South & Western (Agriculture) Ltd, (Incinerators), Great Western Road, Maltock Business Park, Maltock, Somerset TA12 6HB; 01935 826363

Watco (Sales) Ltd, Watco House, Filmer Road, Godalming, Surrey GU7 3AL; 01483 425000

Pet food manufacturers

Beecham Animal Health, Beecham House, Brentford, Middlesex TW8 9BD

B P Nutrition (UK) Ltd, Wincham, Northwich, Cheshire; 01376 513651/01606 41133 (Head Office)

Crown Pet Foods, 72 Green Lane, Vicars Cross, Chester CH3 5LD

Kennel Nutrition, Vitalin Factory, Dallamires Lane, Ripon, North Yorkshire HG4 1TT; 01765 605156

Arden Grange International Ltd, Arden Grange, London Road, Albourne, West Sussex BN6 9BJ; 01273 833390

Pedigree Petfoods, National Office, Waltham on the Wolds, Melton Mowbray, Leicestershire LE14 4RS; 01664 410000

Roberts & Co (Dunchurch) Ltd, 30a Arnold Street, Rugby, Warwickshire CV21 3HD; 01788 579995

Spillers Foods Ltd, Spiller House, 1 Blagdon Road, New Malden, Surrey KT3 4TB; 0181–949 6100

Wafcol Ltd, Whitehill Road, Haigh Avenue, Reddish, Stockport, Cheshire SK4 1NU; 0161–480 2781

Publications

Cats, Our Dogs Publishing Co Ltd, 5 Oxford Road, Station Approach, Manchester M60 2SX; 0161–237 1273

Dogs Monthly, Ascot House, 29A High Street, Ascot, Berkshire SL5 7JG; 01344 28269

Dog World and **Pet Business World,** 9 Tufton Street, Ashford, Kent TN23 1QN; 01233 61877

Kennel and Cattery Management, PO Box 193, Dorking, Surrey RH5 5YF; 01306 712712

Our Dogs, 5 Oxford Road, Station Approach, Manchester M60 2SX; 0161–237 1273

Pet Product Marketing, EMAP Pursuit Publishing Ltd, Bretton Court, Bretton, Peterborough PE3 8DZ; 01733 264666

Miscellaneous

Advisory Conciliation and Arbitration Service (ACAS), 27 Wilton Street, London SW1X 7AZ; 0171–210 3613

Mrs Sheila A Alcock, (Breed Rescue Services), Frogmore Cottage, Kings Walden, Hitchen, Hertfordshire SG4 8NW; 01438 871288

Alliance of Small Firms and Self-Employed People, 42 Vine Road, East Molesey, Surrey KT8 9LF; 0181–979 2293

Animal Health Department, IOM Board of Agriculture & Fisheries, Government Office, Murray House, Mount Havelock, Douglas, Isle of Man; 01624 685845

The Animal Health Trust, PO Box 5, Snailwell Road, Newmarket, Suffolk CB8 7DW

The British Veterinary Association, 7 Mansfield Street, Portland Place, London W1M OT; 0171–636 6541

Animal Care College, RTC Associates, Ascot House, 29A High Street, Ascot, Berkshire SL5 7JG; 01344 28269

Cats Protection League, 17 Kings Road, Horsham, West Sussex RH13 5PN; 01403 221900

Feline Advisory Bureau, Boarding Cattery Officer: Ms Caryl Cruickshank, 1 Church Close, Orcheston, Nr Salisbury, Wiltshire SP3 4RP; 01980 621 201/01747 871872

Governing Council for the Cat Fancy, 4–6 Penel Orlieu, Bridgwater, Somerset TA6 3PG; 01278 427575

Health and Safety Executive, Rose Court, 2 Southwark Bridge, London; 0171–229 3456

HM Customs and Excise, VAT Administration Directorate, New King's Beam House, 22 Upper Ground, London SE1 9PJ; 0171–620 1313

HM Stationery Office, Publication Centre, 51 Nine Elms Lane, London SW8 5DR; 0171–873 0011

Kennel Club, 1 Clarges Street, London W1Y 8AB; 0171–493 6651

National Canine Defence League, 1–2 Pratt Mews, London NW1; 0171–837 0006

Pet Care Trust, Bedford Business Centre, 170 Mile Road, Bedford MK42 9TW

The Pet Trade and Industry Association, Bedford Business Centre, 170 Mile Road, Bedford MK42 9TW; 01234 273933

PRO Dogs, Rocky Bank, 4 New Road, Ditton, Maidstone, Kent ME20 6AD; 01732 848499

Registrar of Companies, Companies House, Crown Way, Maindy, Cardiff CF4 3UZ; 01222 388588

37 Castle Terrace, Edinburgh EH1 2EB; 0131–535 5800

43–47 Chichester Street, Belfast BT1 4RJ; 01232 234121

Royal Society for the Prevention of Cruelty to Animals (RSPCA), The Causeway, Horsham, West Sussex RH12 1HG; 0990 555 999

Rural Development Commission, 141 Castle Street, Salisbury, SP1 3TP; 01722 336255

Further Reading

Croner's Reference Book for the Self-employed and Smaller Business (Croner Publications)

Dog and Cat Nutrition, ed A T B Edney (Pergamon Press)

Encyclopedia of the Cat, Angela Sayer (Octopus)

Starting a Successful Business, M J Morris (Kogan Page)

How to Feed Your Dog, Trevor Turner (Popular Dogs)

Know Your Cat, Geoffrey West (Ventura)

Law for the Small Business, The Daily Telegraph Guide, 8th edn, Patricia Clayton (Kogan Page)

Purnell's Pictorial Encyclopedia of Dogs, Michael Geary (Purnell)

Think Dog, John Fisher (H F & G Witherby)

Understand Your Accounts, 3rd edn, A St J Price (Kogan Page)

Working for Yourself: The Daily Telegraph Guide to Self-employment, 17th edn, Godfrey Golzen (Kogan Page)

Also recommended are the following Feline
Advisory Bureau publications:

Boarding Cattery Construction and Management, S M Hamilton-Moore

Chemical Disinfection in the Cattery, P J Johnson, BVSc, MRCVS

Domestic Toxic Hazards to Cats, Sarah A Wilkins, BVSC, MRCVS

Zoonoses, A I Wright BVSc, MRCVS

Index

Abandoned animals 49, 51
accommodation:
  animal 112–13, 123
  owner's 9, 25–6
  staff 107
accounting 35
  audited accounts 26, 35
  keeping accounts 35, 39
advertising 124–6
alternative medical care 69
Alcock, Sheila 98, 141
Animal Boarding Establishments
  Act *1963* 42–4, 97
animal nursing 13
armed forces 11, 126
arrivals and departures 99
Athag, 121, 139

Bedding materials 54, 63–4, 128
  beds and towels 94–5, 128
boarders 23
boarding capacity 19
boarding cattery 14–15
boarding fees and licences 24, 25, 33,
  38
boarding terms 49
boil-in-the-bag 84
booking application form 49–50, 98
breeding and exhibiting 10
Breeding Dogs Act *1973* 43, 135
British Insurance and Investment
  Brokers Association 34
British Veterinary Association 42–3,
  141
business structure:
  corporation tax 31
  limited company 31
  partnership 30

  sole trader 30
buying an existing business 21–4
buying supplies 40
bylaws 129

Canned food 82
Canine parvovirus disease 73, 135
Cat World 12
Cats 12, 125, 140
Cats Protection League 98, 141
catteries 14–15
  accommodation 23
cesspool and septic tank 65–6
chemical disinfectants 55–60, 76
cheyletiella mange mite 71–2
cleaning routine 91–2
clerical work 10
clothing 67
College of Animal Welfare 41
complete dry diets for dogs and cats
  85–7
complete dry foods 82–3
Compotect 121, 140
construction of kennels 22–3
contract of employment 110–11
creosote 119
Cuprinol 119
Customs and Excise 39, 141

Dangerous dogs 76–8
deep frozen pet foods 84
Department of Agriculture, Dublin 138
Department of Agriculture and
  Fisheries for Scotland 138
destroying worm eggs 70
diabetes 74, 79
Diamond Edge 123, 139
difficult pets 78

Diseases of Animals (Approved Disinfectants) Order *1978* (amended *1991*) 46, 51
distemper 73
District Councils 18–19, 25, 35, 134
DIY 10
Dog Breeders Insurance Co 34, 139
Dog World 12, 21, 125, 141
Dogs Monthly 12, 140
drainage:
    cesspool and septic tank 24

Ear problems 75
eczema 75–6
enquiries, dealing with 100, 126–7
exercise 92
exterior cleaning 61–2
eye problems 76

Feeding Stuffs Regulations *1982* 48, 83
Feline Advisory Bureau 15, 56, 70, 92, 104, 113, 141, 142
feline enteritis 73
feline influenza 73
fencing 119–20
fights 101
financial enquiries 26–7
fire 68
first aid boxes 69
fleas 71, 101
floors 121
food:
    boil-in-the-bag pet foods 84
    canned foods 82
    complete dry diets for dogs and cats 85–7
    complete dry food 82–3
    deep frozen foods 84
    expanded meal 87
    'self-feeding' 88
    semi-moist foods 82
    tripe 84–5
    vacuum packed meats 83–4
formal training:
    Feline Advisory Bureau courses 15

kennel management course 14
Kennel Staff Training Certificate 109
free advice 31–2

Gaining the knowledge 11–12
    dogs shows 12
    specialists publications 11, 12
gates 121–2
getting the best deals 40
Governing Council of the Cat Fancy 128, 141
Groomers Association 96, 133
grooming 96, 109
grooming services 125, 126–7, 133–4, 136

Hardpad 73
health hazards 111
health record cards 95–6
heating 23–4, 95, 122–3
human considerations 67

Immunisations:
    canine parvovirus disease 73
    distemper 73
    feline enteritis 73
    feline influenza 73
    hardpad 73
    kennel cough 74–5
    leptospirosis 73
incineration 65
income 37
income tax and National Insurance 109–10
increased boarding capacity 133
insecticides 60–1
insurance 33–4
isolation units 104

Kennel and Cattery Management 21, 125, 141
kennel buildings 112–23
kennel cleaning 53
    bleach 56–7

chemical disinfectants 55–6
detergent 56
disinfection 54–5
phenol 58
sterilisation of feeding and drinking
bowls 62
tools and equipment 53–4
Kennel Club 142
kennel cough 74–5, 102
kennel inspection 45
kennel kitchen 93–4, 121
kennel staff 106–7
Kennels Agency, The 140
KonKrete Manufacturing Co 139

Lean periods 10
legal restraints 42–51
Leonard, J & A 94
leptospirosis 73
Lever Bros Ltd 57
liability for damage 47
licensing authorities 46–7
loans 29–30
local activities 128–30
local officials 35–6
location:
accessibility 17–18
collection and delivery 18
land values 17
signposted directions 18
house in relation to kennels 25–6
logo 124

Mealtimes 92–3
medication and dangerous substances
74
medicines 102, 104–5
Ministry of Agriculture, Fisheries and
Food (MAFF) 46, 54, 138; for
Northern Ireland 36, 43, 138

National Canine Defence League 13,
142
National Insurance 39, 109
see also income tax

National Kennel Staff Training
Certificate 109
neighbours 25
noise 12, 20, 35, 103
Northern Ireland Local Enterprise
Development Unit 32

Our Dogs 12, 21, 61, 98, 125, 141
outgoings 37–9
running costs 37

Pancreatic problems 74, 79
Pedigree Petfoods 98, 140
pet owners 10, 18
Pet Plan Insurance 34, 139
pollutants 67–8
post mortems 103
practical preparation 10–11
problems with boarders:
aged pets 100–1
bitches in season 101
dangerous dogs 76–8
fights 101
fleas 71, 101
kennel cough 74–5, 102
medicines 102
noise 103
post mortems 103
tail damage 102–3
worms 70–1, 102
product sales, *see* retail trading
professional advice 33
property:
accessibility 17–18
adapting 112
building societies 29
change of use 28
for sale 21
mortgages 29
planning permission 18, 28, 137
public relations 128–30
puppy rearing 135–6

Quarantine kennels 13, 19–20, 43, 54,
136–8

Rabies 70, 111
radio 122
raising finance:
  business plan 29
  government Loan Guarantee Scheme
    29
  loans, private and bank 29
reception 109
reception area 97–9
recommended kennel
  accommodation 113–22
  floors 121
  gates 121–2
  isolation units 120
  kitchens 121
  walls 120
  wooden kennels and cat chalets
    119
refuse collection or burial 66
responsibility 9, 15–16, 106
restrictions on dogs 9–10, 76–8
retail trading 134
rodents 22, 33
Royal Society for the Prevention of
  Cruelty to Animals (RSPCA) 13,
  35–6, 113, 142
RTC Associates 14
running costs 40

Safety first 68
salmonella 72
sarcoptic manage 72
Scottish Business Shop 32
second career 11
security 26, 97, 105, 108, 112–14, 119,
  131
self-employment 9
self-feeding 88
semi-moist foods 82
smells, 12–13, 22
solicitor 32–3
South and Western 140
special diets 79–80
staff training 108–9
staffing 10

starting a new business 20–1
  Environmental Health Officer 20
  licensed kennel 21
  noise problems 12, 20, 103
  planning permission 20, 28, 137
  starting from scratch 21
stationery 127–8
storage 22
stress 12, 63, 75, 79–80

Tail damage 102–3
taking responsibility for animals 15–16
telephone enquiries 126–7
terms for boarding 49–51
tetanus 68–9, 111
toxocariasis 70
toxoplasmosis 71–2
trade sign 124
tripe 84–5

Unlicensed competition 130–1
unpleasant smells and dirty jobs 12–13,
  22

Vacuum packed meats 83–4
value added tax (VAT) 26, 39
veterinary surgeons 11, 13, 18, 104
vitamin C 86
Vortex units 61

Walls 120
Watco (Sales) 121, 140
Welsh Office 138
Wood Green Animal Shelters 113
worms 70, 102

Zoonoses:
  rabies 70; vaccination against 111
  ringworm 70
  salmonella 72
  sarcoptic manage 72
  toxocara canis 70
  toxocara cati 70
  toxocariasis 70
  toxoplasmosis 71–2

Jackal Fence — ⌐ curves inward at top on the perimeter
Dog run attached individual
Large Run spaces
Secure Fenceing system

Smell Control — Natural Cedar, lilac bush research others
shrub   poplars for shade
■ Busiest in the summer months
   25 1person 50 2person
— Kennel 3FT HIGH DIVIDER SOLID topped with wire mess 6 Ft total
— Inside 4 Ft corridor between Kennels is best
— Plastic dividers inside ● removeable

                                                                    ▬ Breeze block
                                                                       with impervious smooth
                                                                       tile surface

— Proper Message Answering Machine
Practice the enquiries part for talking to
prospectie ~~client~~ clients.

— Hot water supply

— max — min thermometers to keep check on heat
— washing machine use definately (can use records my own)
— Cooking, refridge, freezing at my house.

— make sure you build enough space for
an additional Kennel to a max of 40 Kennels

10 10 K MESS   4:30pm main meal
40 Ft   40 F4

① Morning Clean
- let dog into run
- properly wash + sterilize feed dishes
  water
- Floor disinfect
- clean first then disinfect

② Tidy

③ Exercize run rotation as I go along
   the day

④ ~~snack time~~ (Meal)

⑤ rest in full kennels

⑥ Feeding time Afternoon

④ - close in to eat, let rest in small area
   for an hour
   - then clean bowls etc...
   - note who ate and who did not, how much etc.

⑦ Full Kennels

⑧ Play areas

⑨ Full kennel snack

⑩ bedtime close outdoor area

- Own health record card
  Booking Form signed